13218222

WITHDRAWN

Producers Releasing Corporation

For Dennis Coleman
... and his many letters
from Hollywood

and for Gwendolyn Foster
... without whom none of this
might have happened

Producers Releasing Corporation

A Comprehensive Filmography and History

Edited by
Wheeler Dixon

Introduction by
William K. Everson

McFarland & Company, Inc., Publishers
Jefferson, North Carolina, and London

The author gratefully acknowledges those who granted permission to reprint excerpts from the following publications:

Miller, Don. *"B" Movies: An Informal Survey of the American Low Budget Film.* Curtis Books, 1973, New York. Copyright 1973, Film Fan Monthly. Pages 198–208, 301–312, 336–337. Reprinted by kind permission of Leonard Maltin.

Ramsaye, Terry, ed. *1945–46 International Motion Picture Almanac.* Quigley Publishing, 1945, New York. 28 brief biographies excerpted from pages 2, 15, 38, 47, 53, 96, 110, 115, 120, 162, 214, 238, 239, 270, 277, 282, 284, 287, 344, 346, 360, 371, 372, 373, 395, 415, 424, 440, 448, 502. Complete pages: 493–498. Reprinted by permission of publisher.

McCarthy, Todd, and Charles Flynn. *Kings of the "Bs": Working Within the Hollywood System.* E.P. Dutton & Co., 1975, New York. Pages 13–23, 43, and selected filmographies from 508–510, 537–538. Reprinted by permission of publisher.

Everson, William K. *History of the Western Film.* The Citadel Press, 1969, Secaucus, NJ. One paragraph, page 194. (2nd complete paragraph on page.) Reprinted by permission of William K. Everson.

Adams, Les, and Buck Rainey. *Shoot-Em-Ups: The Complete Reference Guide to Westerns of the Sound Era.* Arlington House, 1978, New York. Selected brief filmographies for PRC westerns: pages 212–362. Complete text from pages 257, 258, 342. Reprinted by kind permission of Buck Rainey.

Introduction © 1986 by William K. Everson. All rights reserved.

Edgar G. Ulmer interview, conducted by Peter Bogdanovich. From *Film Culture No. 58–60.* 1970. Copyright © 1974 Peter Bogdanovich. Reprinted by permission of Jonas Mekas, Editor, *Film Culture.*

Library of Congress Cataloguing-in-Publication Data

Producers Releasing Corporation.

   Bibliography: p. 149
   Includes index.
   1. Producers Releasing Corporation (Hollywood, Los Angeles, Calif.) I. Dixon, Wheeler W., 1950– .
PN1999.P76P76 1986   384'.8'06042184   84-43242

ISBN 0-89950-179-6 (acid-free natural paper)

Manufactured in the United States of America

McFarland & Company, Inc., Publishers
  Box 611, Jefferson, North Carolina 28640

Contents

Acknowledgments

I wish to thank William K. Everson for kindly consenting to write an original introductory piece for this volume; his expertise is greatly valued on this project, as always, and the volume is made immeasurably richer by his contribution.

I also would like to thank Leonard Maltin for permission to reprint from Don Miller's *B Movies;* this excellent text has long been out of print, and Mr. Maltin was extremely kind to let me quote from this rare and unfailingly accurate account of PRC's activities. One hopes that the book will be reissued in the near future.

Susan Tiller typed the original manuscript, an enormous task that took six months, and she created a remarkably accurate first draft to work from. My thanks to her. Nancy Ryan completed the typing job, doing her usual excellent work on a difficult project on short notice. Dennis Coleman assisted in digging up hard-to-find information while working full-time as a researcher in Hollywood: his phone calls and letters are certainly reflected in this manuscript.

Wheeler Dixon

Preface

PRC was one of the three biggest "poverty row" studios in Hollywood during the 1940s; the other two were Monogram and Republic. Monogram has received a good deal of favorable critical press in recent years. There are several checklists available, and even a number of critical appraisals of Monogram's feature output. This seems surprising, in view of the fact that Monogram's films were all program pictures — the *Bowery Boys* movies, the *Charlie Chan* films. *Dillinger* (1945), one of the few Monogram films of any distinction, was really the work of the King Brothers, independent producers who brought the project to the studio. The rest of Monogram's films are tedious and technically incompetent. Indeed, the Monogram look is a combination of shoddy sets, dim lighting restricted mostly to simple key spots, nonexistent camerawork (static setups, with simple "master & two-closeups" coverage), and extremely poor sound recording. Monogram optical soundtracks are often so deeply buried in static that it is impossible to understand the dialogue. Jean-Luc Godard, of course, dedicated his first feature, *Breathless*, (1959) to Monogram; perhaps this accounts for some of the company's critical reputation.

Republic's feature output was the slickest of the three studios: crisp, clean photography; a "trick," miniature, and "process" department widely regarded as the best in all of Hollywood (supervised by Howard and Theodore Lydecker, whose work continued into the late 1960s at 20th Century–Fox; their last film was *Our Man Flint*); good "action" music scores (in their rapid, insistent pacing somewhat like the scores Hammer Films would use in the early 1960s); and remarkably fluid camerawork, supervised by cameramen Reggie Lanning and Bud Thackery. Republic's four main house directors (William Witney, John English, Spencer Gordon Bennet, and Joseph Kane) were fond of dollies, extravagant set destruction, and rapid editorial patterning. Features like *Raiders of the Lost Ark* (Paramount, 1981) still attempt to copy the Republic serial style.

But there is not one single book or film checklist in existence on Producers Releasing Corporation, the bottom rung of the studio ladder in 1940s Hollywood: a *cheap* studio, but a very interesting studio, as well. Unlike Monogram, which ground out *Bowery Boys* programmers and

Charlie Chan thrillers in a predictable, monotonous fashion, and Republic, which specialized mostly in serials and formula "action" features, PRC produced, in addition to a large number of quota quickies, a series of arresting and occasionally important films which have never been fully discussed. As the first book on PRC, this text is no more than a preliminary stab at the complete output of the studio.

Special attention is paid in this volume to two of PRC's more important directors: Edgar G. Ulmer, well known but appreciated more for his *Black Cat* for Universal (1934) than for his 1940s PRC films (*Detour*, 1945; *Strange Illusion*, 1945; *Club Havana*, 1945; *Isle of Forgotten Sins*, 1943; *Bluebeard*, 1944; and many others, discussed at length in this text); and Sam Newfield, aka Sherman Scott and Peter Stewart, one of the more mysterious figures in film history. While Ulmer has acquired a certain backhanded "camp" notoriety (Andrew Sarris in *The American Cinema:* "Yes, Virginia, there *is* an Edgar G. Ulmer"), practically no information exists on Newfield, who directed more than fifty films for PRC from 1939–1947. One of the major reasons for writing this book was to get *some* information on Newfield in print, other than the fact that he was Sigmund Neufeld's (head of PRC) brother.

It is very, very difficult to get information on PRC's feature output. The filmographies included in this volume are as accurate as we could make them. If we have omitted a film, we hope readers will call the error to our attention.

The films of PRC occupy a peculiar niche in film history. Grouping by "genre," PRC westerns are generally miserable and not worth any discussion. They inhabit a sort of cinematic twilight zone, as the *cheapest* of the cheap features that PRC produced. The average shooting schedule for a PRC film was five days. Many of the westerns were shot in two or three.

PRC musicals, except those directed by Edgar Ulmer (like *Club Havana*, 1945, and *Jive Junction*, 1943) are also not worthy of sustained examination. Most are glittering tacky packages of third-rate stars, with fifth-rate music.

But PRC mysteries, dramas, and action films are something else again: bitter, hard-edged, straight-to-the-point.

Although circumstances at PRC were financially perilous, the low budgets and ultrashort shooting schedules afforded a certain personal creative freedom, which directors like Ulmer, Newfield (and to a lesser extent, Christy Cabanne) capitalized on. No one really cared what was "in the can," as long as you had at least fifty-four minutes of programming. The films were sold on *titles*, backed up by sensationalized press materials, in the time-honored "B" picture fashion. They were distributed through a tenuous "States' Rights" network, which allowed extremely marginal profit-per-picture to the studio: about $1750 a picture by PRC's own in-house estimate. Because of this, PRC was stuck in low-budget production;

they would never produce a film that became a "sleeper," a film made on a modest budget which achieves great critical or box office success. PRC films are works of desperation; at times, exquisite desperation. The first take will probably be the only take. The lines are read off cue-cards: out of shot, sometimes *in* the shot. Whenever possible, actual locales are used. Sets are rigorously minimal. Most of PRC's seventy-five-minute films were shot on a ratio of 1½ to 1; about one hundred minutes of raw stock for a finished feature of sixty to eighty minutes running time. (PRC westerns were usually fifty-four minutes; other "genre" films had to be longer.) Back-projection was used whenever possible; why build an entire ballroom set at great expense, when you can rear-project the ballroom as a background behind a few actors?

The cheapness of the physical execution in all PRC films has worked against any accurate evaluation of the studio's output. While the glossier approach of the majors won greater contemporary public favor, PRC's neorealist, "No Way Out" vision has acquired a resonance over the last thirty years that few major productions can equal. An evaluation of PRC productions pits Joseph Kane against John Ford; Edgar Ulmer against Curtiz, Mankiewicz, Wilder, and Hawks. In Ford's leisurely Old West, a patina of sentiment clouds the imagery. In Joseph Kane's westerns such as *Brimstone*, 1949 (actually made by Republic, but very close in spirit to PRC's late 1940s westerns), there is no such thing as a "Code of the West," or a sense of historical perspective. Everything is immediate, vicious, do-or-die. All dialogue is reduced to motivation, rather than speculative analysis by the characters, as in many of Ford's westerns (particularly his later, self-indulgent efforts such as *She Wore a Yellow Ribbon*, 1949). Joseph Kane's films are works of the moment, operating on the level of the protagonists, *of* their world. It is this quality which distinguishes the best "B" film — a film made with certain restrictions, but with certain priorities also established. *Detour*, for example, succeeds because it fully acknowledges its miserable surroundings and insists on their authenticity. Many of PRC's features *are* miserable: cheap in every respect and utterly worthless. Mixed in with the junk, though, is something quite remarkable.

Wheeler Dixon

Introduction:
Remembering PRC

by William K. Everson

The only way to *reliably* remember PRC is to have seen all its films when they came out, in the context of their period, and in juxtaposition to product from the other companies. This has both disadvantages and advantages, the latter largely in that we were seeing PRC films at their pristine best, in good new 35mm release prints, not in the largely tattered and often badly duped prints that survive today and are often considered adequate for the cable channels specializing in public domain material that doesn't have to be paid for.

Also, since we're going back forty-five years in time, it should be remembered that those of us who now consider ourselves historians were then youngsters interested primarily in being entertained. Certainly there were those of us who took more than a casual interest in film, and could be excited when PRC came up with an interesting script or a good director, but basically we tended to dismiss PRC as being beneath contempt. It was quite a game among schoolboys to come up with the most insulting uses of the PRC initials to describe their product.

This attitude apparently still prevails. It's interesting that there were several full-page advertisements in *Variety* early in 1985 offering the PRC product for resale here and abroad — but because of the stigma attached to the name, never once admitting that they were in fact PRC pictures.

Poor PRC in a sense got caught in the middle. Due to rising costs, many of the cheap independent producers like Bernie B. Ray and Maurice Conn were being phased out of production in the late 1930s. But there was still a need for product of that type, and PRC supplied it. Moreover, the fact that it was a new company meant that it got a certain amount of attention and even a few reviews — which, written by critics totally unfamiliar with the "B" market, could hardly be favorable.

When PRC got underway, all the majors were still making expert little "B" films — not so much directed at the action market as they were at

1

providing supports for their own "A"s, so that the whole program could be sold on percentage. Warners, Fox, MGM (whose "B"s all looked like "A"s), Universal, and RKO were all turning out extremely slick little pictures, and of course all had the benefits of big contract lists of stars and directors, standing sets, and huge backlogs of stock footage, all of which could add production values to their smaller pictures. Some of Paramount's "B"s (such as *Buy Me That Town, Among the Living* and *Dr. Broadway*) were quite superior to their average run of "A" movies. But when it comes down to the action market at which PRC was primarily aimed, audiences tended to make comparisons not between a PRC and a Fox, but between a PRC and films from those other action studios, Republic and Monogram.

There is no question that Republic turned out the best product of the three. Their camerawork (often by masters like John Alton) was sharp, clear and bright. The fights and chases were superbly well choreographed, the stunts of a high order, and Republic had made enough moderately-budgeted "specials" to have a good supply of useful stock footage on hand.

Monogram approached the Republic gloss, but turned out a very bland product, avoiding action wherever possible. Films with promising titles like *Gang Bullets* turned out to be literally all talk. The Monograms were polished enough not to flaunt their cheapness too obviously, but most of them were dull, and it was rare that one wanted to see a Monogram a second time. (I worked for Monogram in the early 1950s and had the opportunity, of which I certainly availed myself, to rescreen scores of their "B"s from the 1930s and 1940s — and how I wished I were working instead for the then-defunct PRC!)

But PRC films did have a special quality, and even if audiences didn't knowingly differentiate between a Monogram and a PRC, I think that subliminally that difference did have an effect.

My own recollection of the PRCs (confirmed by more recent reviewings) is of how dank and dark most of them were. Interior sets were often so threadbare that the lighting was deliberately kept low to hide the fact that there was really nothing to look at. An Edgar Ulmer could answer the challenge and turn darkness into a film noir asset, but many directors couldn't. Also, most of the street scenes (whether the locale was Europe, New York, or points in between) were shot in the immediate studio environs, and again were underlit so that the patently Hollywood backgrounds weren't too apparent. Somehow the habit of underlighting spilled over to the westerns too, where long chase sequences were for some reason shot at night, totally obliterating the action that the youngsters paid to see. However, even here, there were occasionally logical reasons for the lack of visibility. In *Outlaws of Boulder Pass*, the supposedly dead but very much alive Dennis Moore has to climb back into his grave to be there in the event that the villains decide to check on him. They do; and

Jack La Rue (left) has to get tough with Richard Deane in "Swamp Woman."

the pitch-black lighting spares us the details of his unlikely masquerade, as well as presumably preventing the villains from wondering why the long-dead body isn't in a more advanced state of decomposition!

I think what gives distinction, if that is the right word, to the PRC films is that they really *tried*. Knowing that they had zero production values to offer, no great pool of art directors and writers to fall back on, certainly no impressive vault filled with stock footage, they tried to make up for it with ingenuity and a certain amount of window dressing. Erich von Stroheim, Elissa Landi, Otto Kruger, John Carradine, Lionel Atwill, Bela Lugosi, Anna May Wong, Richard Arlen and Buster Crabbe were just a few of the quite respectable names that they used to advantage. Crabbe's three Jungle films (*Jungle Man*, *Jungle Siren* and *Nabonga*) were not likely to give the MGM Tarzans much competition — but at least each one was better than its predecessor, and all of them were infinitely superior to a Monogram turkey of the same period, *Law of the Jungle*.

Much of the raw vitality (and that's a quality the Monograms never had) comes from PRC's use of interesting directors on their way up (Joseph H. Lewis in particular), writers of promise (Carl Foreman) and veteran directors who often performed above and beyond the call of duty just to show that they could still deliver (William K. Howard, or the German directors Frank Wysbar and Douglas Sirk, refugees from Europe who were starting all over again). Sometimes, and doubtless without the PRC higher-ups knowing what was going on, these directors got away with near miracles of innovation. For example, Lewis's *Secrets of a Co-Ed* comes to its climax with a courtroom scene done in one dazzling ten-minute take — this almost a decade before Alfred Hitchcock's *Rope*.

Perhaps because they had so few of them, PRC directors knew the value of a dollar. Apart from stretching them as far as they'd go, they also tried to see that every dollar spent actually showed up on the screen. Let's compare, for example, Universal's *Raiders of the Desert* (1941) with PRC's *Bombs Over Burma* (1942). Both were unpretentious little pictures aimed at the same market. Universal was content to grind it out efficiently (using some nice standing sets to add gloss) so that the action fans would go home happy. PRC, on the other hand, tried to add that little bit extra so that audiences other than the action crowd would be happy with it. In *Raiders of the Desert*, Universal made no attempt at all to suggest an Arabian locale. It was all shot in the foothills at the back of the studio, with nary a grain of Arabian sand shown until the climax, which was all nonmatching stock lifted from an earlier John Wayne "B", *I Cover the War*. Universal also had the temerity to have the one movie theatre in their thriving little desert town showing the two Universal "B"s — *Mug Town* and *Law and Order*. (At least there are no lines outside the box office!) In *Bombs Over Burma*, however, the ubiquitous Joseph H. Lewis managed to turn out a pocket von Sternberg, adding exotic lighting to the virtually nonexistent sets, or framing much of the action through the wheels of a rickshaw. At one point his camera zeroes into a closeup of a back-projected stock footage, then pulls *back* into the interior of a car, which takes off — the back projection rapidly receding into infinity.

PRC really knew the value of its stars, too, and perhaps another side-by-side comparison with Universal is not inappropriate. In one of the cheater come-ons of all time, Bela Lugosi and Lionel Atwill (both contract players) share star billing in the opening credit of Universal's *The Night Monster*. Neither of them has anything to do, though it would have been a simple matter to switch them to the key roles played by Nils Asther and Ralph Morgan. Even if Atwill was to be a red herring, they could have dignified his presence by making him the *last* victim to be killed off; instead, he is the first. PRC made no such mistakes in its *Fog Island* a couple of years later; PRC had *paid* for Atwill and George Zucco, and those actors were going to *work* before they went home to supper. As if knowing that this was going to be no cheater (though admittedly no masterpiece either) the writers seemed to work overtime coming up with little extra scenes and lines to exploit what by PRC standards was an all-star cast. When towards the end, with George Zucco's booty about to be discovered, Ian Keith slides out of the shadows to demand his share, Atwill somewhat huffily

Stock footage of an actual fire was used in this scene from PRC's "Arson Squad."

asks him why. "I know where the bodies are buried" replies Keith with a good-natured smile, and Atwill abruptly changes the subject!

Perhaps it is mainly in the westerns that the legendary cheapness of PRC shows up most. Westerns were still economical to make in the early forties, and one could come up with a fairly streamlined product for a very modest budget. But production costs rose while income remained static. Some companies, especially RKO, upped their budgets drastically to retain the quality they were proud of, even though it meant a smaller return. PRC, however, kept its budgets on the same level, turning out a shoddier product, but hoping to get the same return. The earlier PRC westerns tend to be the best — those with stars like Tim McCoy and Buster Crabbe (felicitously teamed with Al St. John), whose personas somehow dominated the westerns to the degree that the films at least had a little more plot and motivation. The later ones, apart from being hurt by the decidedly nonmusical scores of Lee Zahler and Frank Sanucci, also suffered from poor direction — with veteran Elmer Clifton (who never quite duplicated the one fluke classic of his silent years, *Down to the Sea in Ships*) and Sam Newfield giving the films no style at all. "Motivation"

Felix Bressart (center) runs a swinging cabaret in New Orleans in "Her Sister's Secret."

was often limited to Holly Bane or Charles King walking into a saloon, spotting Buster Crabbe and saying "I don't like your face, stranger." Crabbe would understandably take umbrage, and the scrap would be on — to be followed by a plot similarly light in dramatic structure. PRC was also singularly unfortunate in winding up with some of the least suitable western stars. George Houston just never seemed at home in the West, and the flat hats he wore merely stressed how uncomfortable he was. And "Lash" La Rue is a star that should never have been perpetrated on *any* company making westerns, not even Ajax, Resolute, or Reliable.

PRC put characteristic effort into its attempts to break into the "A" market, although there perhaps Monogram did have better success. Too often the money went on production and not on stars. Martin Kosleck was nobody's idea of a swashbuckling Edmond Dantes in *The Wife of Monte Cristo*, and good and intelligent though *Her Sister's Secret* was, it was hurt by that poor title and the fact that it couldn't hope to compete with the big Stanwyck and Davis specials that Warner was making at the same time. No, PRC was at its best when it had very little — and relied on Edgar Ulmer and Joseph H. Lewis to make it look like far more.

There are many PRCs that I have no wish to see again and could cheerfully forget (if they weren't too awful to be forgotten) — films like *My Son, the Hero, Duke of the Navy,* and *Misbehaving Husbands.* But against those and their ilk, one can point to *Strange Illusion, Strangler of the Swamp, Minstrel Man, Bluebeard* and many others of fond remembrance — and genuine merit, if regarded in the right perspective.

It's good that PRC should have a book devoted to its short, busy life. The company deserves it.

PRC Chronology

1938:   Ben Judell forms Progressive Pictures Corporation (PPC).

1939:   PPC becomes Producers Distributing Corporation (PDC).

1940:   Financial crisis. March: PDC becomes Sigmund Neufeld Productions. November: SNP becomes Producers Releasing Corporation, formed as a subsidiary of Pathé Laboratories, Inc., with O. Henry Briggs as president.

1943:   PRC Pictures, Inc., new name of Producers Releasing Corporation (PRC).

1946:   April: Eagle-Lion Studios new name for PRC Studios.

1947:   August: PRC completely absorbed by Eagle-Lion, with Arthur Krim as president.

1950:   January: Film Classics merged with Eagle-Lion.

1951:   February: Eagle-Lion merged into UA; Arthur Krim becomes UA president.

A Brief History of
Producers Releasing Corporation

by Don Miller

Whatever PRC may have lacked in professional skills or artistic flair, there's no denying that they had some definite ideas on how a movie should be merchandised, and that this merchandising enabled them to persevere through some quite awful productions. But it was difficult to dislike PRC pictures, just as it was not easy to find a few kind words within one's heart for them. Defects abounded in every department. Performances would rate with a high school dramatics society under stress. Direction would consist of pointing the camera in a particular area and shouting "Action!" and hoping for the best; and the camera, when pointed, might be out of focus. Sets would shimmy and shake if an actor slammed a door upon entering. The editing would involve repetition of certain pieces of film, presumably because there was no covering footage. Sound recording was terrible — music, straight out of the can.

But the stories, or the titles, or something — there was always something to sell. And eventually, PRC would occasionally turn out a perfectly respectable film.

Even its origins were shrouded in false starts. When founded by Ben Judell in 1939, it was referred to as Producers Pictures. After its first couple of releases it became known as Producers Distributing Corporation. A few further films, and it was Producers Releasing Corporation, shortened to PRC.

Shepard Traube had written a story of life inside Nazi Germany entitled *Goose Step*. Producers bought it and scheduled it as their first film. In the light of the world situation, especially after September 1, 1939, the title was changed to the more dynamic *Hitler — Beast of Berlin*. It was shown to the trade under this title. Subsequently it became *Beasts of Berlin*, but as public sentiment mounted in favor of the Allied cause, the Hitler title became prominent on the marquees and lobby posters, even though the title might have been softened on the screen. But at first, at the time of its official release date of October 15, 1939, it was a "hot" item. Ar-

9

tistically it was not so hot, but this was of secondary concern. The New York board of censors took a look at it, considered the sensibilities of the various Bund camps prevalent in New York and nearby New Jersey, tallied the possibilities, and banned the film. After a month's hesitation, which saw the title changed to the less inflammatory one, and some censorial cuts that seemed little more than arbitrary, it finally opened in New York City on November 18. In more of a patriotic gesture than a display of critical common sense, the reviewers generally praised the intent of the film, refraining as best they could from remarking on the numerous technical and artistic faults.

Not that *Beasts of Berlin* was a downright disaster. Its sincerity was apparent and unquestioned, and there were a good many things in it that were presented on the screen for the first time; some became clichés through repetition in subsequent anti–Nazi films and some were vitiated by clumsy exposition, but things were said that had to be said. And it was the first fiction feature to depict an interpretation of what was going on inside Hitler's Third Reich.

Basically, the story centered on an underground group passing out propaganda against the Nazis, of how they were detected and captured, imprisoned in a concentration camp, and how their leader (Roland Drew) and his wife (Steffi Duna) eventually escaped (distressingly easily) to Switzerland, where presumably they would carry on the fight for freedom in their homeland. Counterbalancing the frequent naivete of the narrative, many scenes were strongly delivered and compelling in their honesty. One curious result of the censors' trepidation came when a Nazi bigwig scans a news headline announcing President Roosevelt's lend-lease policy to the Allies, and snaps: "Meddling fool!" The exclamation was muddied and distorted on the sound track of the print seen in its first New York run, as if the censors didn't want to see any display of disapproval. Their fears were groundless, for increasing fervor on behalf of the Allies and the sharp decrease in popularity of the local Bundists and quasi–Nazis nullified any serious thoughts of reprisals.

Controversial in a way that was good for the box office, the film probably returned a healthy profit on its economical budget outlay. It continued to be profitable for PRC, or whoever became its distributor in years to come, and then not because of its topicality. A featured player named Alan Ladd had become a tremendous box office draw from the early 1940s onward, and since he had been laboring in the Hollywood fields for a long time as a performer in sundry low-budget films, many of them would naturally be trotted out to cash in on his name. So it was with Producers' first; in time it became known as *Hell's Devils*, with Ladd's name billed in huge letters above the title, to snare the unwary who might think it was a brand-new movie. Since stills of Ladd were relatively scarce in scenes from the film, ingenuity overcame honest instincts. A still showing Roland Drew undergoing the rigors of torture in the concentration camp, dragged half-conscious back to his cell, was tampered with and the actor's face replaced with an insert of Ladd's, suitably battered and begrimed, on the theory that since Ladd's name was now on top, he should be the recipient of the punishment meted out only to those of star status.

Producers Pictures' second release hardly possessed the ringing box-office values of the first, although some effort was made to exploit the name of Jack London as author of the original story, *A Thousand Deaths.* But *Torture Ship*, as it was called, was nothing but a seedy crook melodrama, more than a trifle foolish in its overacting and limp direction by Victor Halperin, negating any possibility of making something out of the tale about a mad doctor (Irving Pichel) who does some fiendish experimenting on a group of criminals aboard a yacht. Lyle Talbot did the heroics, Jacqueline Wells the cringing. Halperin directed the third 1939 release — and by now it was clearly established that the company was Producers Distributing — and failed to improve the mediocre level with *Buried Alive*, a prison yarn with all the frayed trimmings: hero (Robert Wilcox) condemned for a crime he didn't commit, prison nurse (Beverly Roberts) who stands by him, trickery to obtain a last-minute confession from the guilty, and other foreseeable plot machinations.

The Invisible Killer, the last 1939 release, was a girl-reporter–frustrated-detective murder mystery played by Grace Bradley and Roland Drew. Drew, hero of *Beasts of Berlin*, was again directed by Sherman Scott, the same Sherman Scott who was to direct westerns with Bob Steele and Buster Crabbe. The same director would in time do western series with Tim McCoy and George Houston, using the name of Peter Stewart. Should the names Sherman Scott and Peter Stewart be meaningless to movie buffs, they might be more familiar with the name of Sam Newfield, a long-time poverty-row director: Mr. Newfield assumed the two pseudonyms for his work.

The Peter Stewart division of Sam Newfield's psyche directed the first and last in what was hoped to be a series of westerns featuring a twelve-year-old in the lead, Bobby Clark (definitely no relation to the celebrated stage buffoon). *The Sagebrush Family Trails West* had Master Clark, Earle Hodgins, Minerva Urecal and Joyce Bryant mired in a story about a traveling medicine show, with the usual banditry tangent thrown in. Young Clark sat a horse like a true son of the prairie and swung a wide loop with his lariat. But the thought of a Hardy family on horseback was a bit too much to contemplate, especially since William Lively's script failed to dignify his last name and Peter Stewart's direction was a shade below Sherman Scott's best work.

While Scott-Stewart-Newfield was involved in other matters, Richard Harlan directed *Mercy Plane*, with the skidding James Dunn and the stylishly attractive Frances Gifford. Harlan normally brought home the paychecks through his work as assistant or second-unit director. *Mercy Plane* remains his only opportunity to do a full feature, and as such

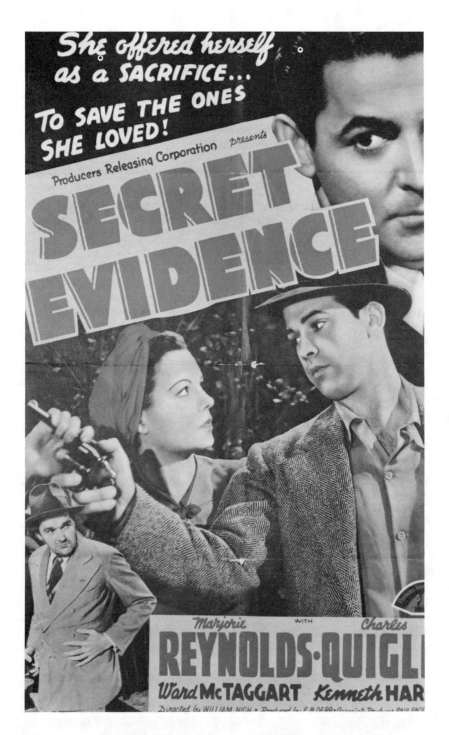

PRC's "Secret Evidence" was an underworld melodrama.

was passable, although the story of plane thefts and an amazing new-fangled craft that rises from the ground like a helicopter was hard to swallow and the juvenile special effects work did nothing to make it believable. *Mercy Plane* was released in February 1940, and for a time bid well to be last on the list of releases from the new company. Wobbly and not fulfilling their schedule, Producers Distributing Corporation seemed headed for that happy indie hunting ground populated by Victory, Puritan, Reliable and the rest of the little companies of yore.

In May 1940 came *I Take This Oath*, an unmemorable cops-and-robbers concoction about a policeman's son (Gordon Jones) out to avenge the death of his father, not materially different from the hordes of "B" police pictures preceding it, routine in performance, writing and Sherman Scott's direction. But it represented the first release from the revivified, renourished, and renamed Producers Releasing Corporation. The following month, *Hold That Woman!* was ready for exhibition. James Dunn and Frances Gifford were reteamed (they were husband and wife offscreen) in a flippant comedy about "skip-tracers," or those leeches whose job it is to collect from runouts on installment payments. No great shakes, but it offered Dunn more opportunity to display his impudent charm than did his preceding effort. Inevitably, Sherman Scott directed. Two months later, at the end of August, *Marked Men* appeared. Warren Hull and Isabel Jewell led the cast of an uninspired tale of an escaped convict trying to carve a new life. Scott directed without any noticeable spark, all too understandable considering the amount of labor he had put in during the past year.

Sam Newfield (aka Sherman Scott/Peter Stewart), under producer Sigmund Neufeld (they were brothers), directed the vast majority of PRC's releases during its unsteady formative period. They had assembled enough Tim McCoy and Bob Steele westerns to fill in the schedule to some extent, while the newly vitalized PRC company retrenched for a few months. The next nonwestern PRC feature came in December 1940. In fact, two were released practically simultaneously, neither of them from the Neufeld-Newfield factory.

The Devil Bat was, as its title implies, a horror film, produced by Jack Gallagher and directed by Jean Yarbrough. *Misbehaving Husbands* was produced by Jed Buell, directed by William Beaudine. It was a domestic comedy with Harry Langdon, while the horror film starred Bela Lugosi. Neither amounted to much artistically, but each had selling angles, which had not been abundant in the last several PRC releases. The exploitative values in the Lugosi film are obvious, while *Misbehaving Husbands* marked the return to feature-length comedies of Langdon, once vying with Chaplin for popularity and whose screen career plummeted as swiftly as it had ascended. After many sad years in short slapstick comedies and small to medium parts in features, Langdon once more topped the cast in a vehicle of his own.

Neil Hamilton (center) is about to get roughed up in this scene from "Federal Fugitives."

Langdon was good. His role was not unique in the way that his silent-film character was; he played an innocent accused by his wife (Betty Blythe) of cheating after twenty years of marriage, and the consequences of the accusation involve a near-divorce. There were a few laughs in the part, but Langdon reached into his bag of cinema tricks and extracted a number of additional chuckles with his timed reactions to a distressing turn of plot, and occasional hints of the babyish characteristics inherent in his presound portrayals.

William Beaudine's direction was also helpful. Beaudine's career dated back to the dawn of film history. At various times he had directed Mary Pickford, W.C. Fields and sundry bright lights of the golden days. He had journeyed to England in the mid-1930s for a stint, only to be given "B" films of the Torchy Blane series variety upon his return. *Misbehaving Husbands* was the first of a staggering number of "B" indie films made by Beaudine during the next two decades. Its cast was also more interesting than the average indie "B" pic; in addition to Langdon and Miss Blythe, there were Ralph "Dick Tracy" Byrd, blonde vamp Esther Muir, smooth-voiced Gayne Whitman, appealing Luana Walters, and a young man with a future named Byron Barr, later to become Gig Young.

Lugosi's ups and downs in films are inexplicable. Predating Boris Karloff in horror films with his Dracula portrayal, the Hungarian actor evidently received faulty advice on which roles to accept, or was in some other way victimized. When Karloff was mired in inferior material, at least he persevered and maintained his dignity, usually lending the turkey what little worthiness it possessed. Lugosi, however, would be frequently completely overcome by the ineptitudes of his part, becoming a caricature of his intentions and thereby lowering his own standards. He had given a legitimately expert performance in *Son of Frankenstein* (1939) as the crazed peasant Ygor, but apparently was unable to take advantage of this success. He was back with his mad-scientist routine in *The Devil Bat*, and he had gone through the motions of the role countless times before in low-budget features and serials.

Producers Releasing Corporation was now living up to its name as 1941 commenced. Ted Richmond, E.B. Derr, John T. Coyle, Martin Mooney and others were now readying economically-made features for the company, with Sig Neufeld continuing to supervise the western output. But although the flow of films was steady, it rapidly became apparent that PRC was not going to enter any product in contention for Academy Awards. It was the old story indigenous to indies, a combination of newcomers on the way up, old-timers on the way down, with no middle ground on which to meet and consolidate their talents. The first four 1941 releases seemed to exemplify this status by alternating means.

Caught in the Act was an alleged comedy toplining Henry Armetta as a construction foreman mixed up with crooks and blondes. Armetta was amusing in small, or featured doses, but carrying the load of an entire feature without support, as he had in his 20th–Fox Sports Series, was too much to ask.

Secret Evidence was primarily a showcase for Marjorie Reynolds, on the rise from extra girl to western ingenue to indie lead. Miss Reynolds was competent, and would in fact receive her ticket to stardom playing opposite Bing Crosby and Fred Astaire a few years hence. But the film was stodgy, silly in its underworld melodramatics and not aided by the direction of William Nigh, moving over from Monogram for a brief spell.

Federal Fugitives was about government agents on the trail of a foreign spy ring and had Neil Hamilton in the lead, with Victor Varconi and Betty Blythe prominently featured, all of them names from filmdom's past. The ingenue was Doris Day, and it is mandatory to add, not the singer Doris Day who became the screen's richest professional virgin. Another Doris Day is the inapt but unavoidable way of putting it.

Emergency Landing had Forrest Tucker in the hero's role. Tucker was a recent arrival in the movies and at this time known primarily as the recipient of a thrashing from Gary Cooper in last year's Goldwyn epic *The Westerner*, and offscreen as an escort of some of the most glamorous starlets in Hollywood and a professional golfer in ability. Carol Hughes, ingenue, had been in movies for a few years but was still considered a new

"Desperate Cargo" featured more fisticuffs than attention to detail: Note clapper board still on café table, lower left corner of bottom photo. Ralph Byrd (facing left in both photos) is the natty slugger.

face. Billed third was Evelyn Brent, still as smokily exotic as in her days
at Paramount with von Sternberg. Far down in the cast was Jack
Lescoulie, who became one of the big television names as an announcer.
None of these four films had ambitions beyond their supporting-feature
niche and none achieved further fame.

South of Panama had the likable Roger Pryor and some moderately
witty dialogue by Ben Roberts and Sidney Sheldon, woven into a spy script
that was not taken seriously, especially by its writers. *Paper Bullets*
belongs outside the realm because of several factors and will be discussed
later.

Criminals Within was one of the few films of the period to deal with
draftees—the draft had gone into effect in October 1940. *Double Cross*
had the winsomely pretty Pauline Moore, whose last film it proved to be,
and a crime yarn guaranteed to excite no one. *Desperate Cargo* was an
adventure whose shoestring budget must have been frayed before production from the look of the sets. However it had a pleasant cast: Ralph Byrd,
Carol Hughes, Jack Mulhall, Kenneth Harlan, and an intriguing girl
named Julie Duncan. Miss Duncan was not in the standard Hollywood
glamour tradition, possessing instead a wholesomeness and sincerity, gar-
nished by a distinctive speaking voice, that smacked of good roles to come.
She had been seen in a number of westerns and was more than convincing
because of her riding prowess. *Desperate Cargo* was her best part to date,
despite its production deficiencies, and she made her ingenue part count
for more than it was worth. As ill fortune would have it, the talent agents
and executive scouts were all apparently looking in another direction. She
eventually drifted out of films.

Gambling Daughters had a spicy come-on in its advertising but was
nothing more than a crime story, complete with mysteriously unidentified
"boss." Besides, romantic leads Cecilia Parker and Robert Baldwin were
man and wife in real life, so it was almost a family film. *Reg'lar Fellers*
was based on the comic strip and featured Billy Lee and Carl "Alfalfa"
Switzer; if PRC had intended to develop the characters into a series, they
were stymied by the lack of quality in the opener.

With autumn, PRC seemed to put slightly more effort into their
releases. Made cheaply but surprisingly entertaining was a mystery of the
"Thin Man" school, *Dangerous Lady,* with Neil Hamilton as a private eye
and June Storey as his wife, a lawyer. The repartee between them, and
with the frustrated cop, Douglas Fowley, was slightly superior to the
norm, Hamilton gave a good impression of enjoying himself, Bernard B.
Ray had not directed as competent a film before, nor did he later. Most
felicitous was the background music by Clarence Wheeler. The composer
obviously was restricted to a motley assortment of musicians, but he overcame this with some jaunty airs that the salon group played with
lilt.

Before taking over from Bob Steele in the "Billy the Kid" western

(Top) Mary Healy picks up some loose change in "Hard Guy," then (bottom) reluctantly hands it over to Jack La Rue.

series, Buster Crabbe was finagled into a final jungle fling replete with loin-cloth and stuffed lions. *Jungle Man* was produced by Ted Richmond, directed by Harry Fraser, and enacted by Crabbe and fellow thespians in what appeared to be someone's backyard. Actually, Crabbe played a doctor looking for a cure for jungle fever, but found reason and opportunity to strip down for the occasion. The photographer, Mervyn Freeman, was also credited as associate producer, no doubt a tip-off on the economies of the film.

Hard Guy was an exploitation effort with Mary Healy, formerly of the 20th–Fox musicals, playing earnestly as a cigarette girl in order to find the murderer of her sister, with Jack La Rue in the cast. Elmer Clifton directed, and the results were slightly above Clifton's indies of the thirties. *Mr. Celebrity* was an innocuous family drama about an orphan (Buzzy Henry), horseracing and heartaches, with a built-in gimmick of having three senior citizens — Francis X. Bushman, Clara Kimball Young, and former boxing champ Jim Jeffries — make brief appearances. William Beaudine directed, as he did the following PRC release, *The Miracle Kid*, a comedy about a boxer (Tom Neal) involved with some health nuts. Neal showed muscular biceps for the ladies, Carol Hughes appeared to advantage in a bathing suit for the lads, and nobody was particularly offended.

With year's end in sight, PRC hit hard with their potential box office bonanza, most promising since their initial release. It also proved to be one of their worst films, one of the most inept films of the year, or of any other year. Since Gypsy Rose Lee had made some small success by forsaking her art as an ecdysiast, striptease, or in burlesque parlance peeler, to become an actress, her sisters in the profession had entertained similar ambitions. Latest to give it a try was Ann Corio, who had made a statuesque Tondelayo in a legit production of *White Cargo* (MGM). Now it was Miss Corio's turn to display her talents. Arthur G. Durlam had prepared a screenplay for producers George Merrick and Max Alexander; and those gentlemen, in league with director Elmer Clifton, duly committed the work to celluloid. *Swamp Woman* was a soufflé about a dancer (Miss Corio), a ratty promoter (Jay Novello), an escaped convict (Richard Deane), a pursuing policeman (Ian MacDonald), the dancer's nubile niece (Mary Hull) and her intended (Jack La Rue), all floundering together in the bayou country. The stringiness of this heady mulligatawny was supposedly compensated for by its conclusion wherein all strands are disposed of — the convict is really innocent because the ratty promoter is the true culprit, the niece gets the convict, and her former fiancé goes for the dancer. As if the plot outline isn't woeful enough, the attendant technical and artistic aspects are even more mournful, including acting and dialogue hardly worthy of a company on tour in the backwoods; nonexistent direction; dark photography that managed to detract from Miss Corio's prominent charms; seedy production values. Miss Corio gave a

Jack La Rue and Ann Curio (center) engage in a bit of rural entertainment in "Swamp Woman."

performance that showed her capable of delivering lines, with the rest questionable in view of the material. La Rue looked painfully embarrassed, with the rest of the cast following suit, intentionally or otherwise. Bad as the movie was, it nevertheless had the drawing power to play profitably in the shooting-gallery houses and exploitation havens, who weren't getting too much in the way of hot product at the time. Miss Corio was also signed for more films, by the reasoning that the droll debacle was not her fault.

Swamp Woman was officially released on Friday, December 5, 1941.

PRC's last release of 1941, Law of the Timber, had producer-director Bernard B. Ray resorting to his old stock-in-trade, a James Oliver Curwood story. But the Curwood authorship no longer meant as much as it did for the movies, and the film itself used techniques harkening back to the days of the early-sound indies, and even on that score would suffer by comparison. Cast with Marjorie Reynolds winning top billing by default, the only dependable males among the featured players were Monte Blue and J. Farrell MacDonald; the hero was portrayed by a Hal Brazeal. Doubles used for the fisticuffing scenes were all too obvious. What the hero lacked in thespic ability he atoned for in physique, which was definitely not that of his stuntman's, who was rotund and more than a bit paunchy

Top: A typical scene of Crime in the Big City, from "Today I Hang" (Mona Barrie, center). Bottom: Things don't look good for Walter Wolf King (center) in "Today I Hang."

(as well as punchy, from the way he threw them). In an ill-advised attempt to inject some outdoor excitement, a logging train being dynamited was achieved, but the model work was so inept it looked like a display window in a toy store.

William Beaudine, a resourceful director under normal conditions and even under stress, turned out two alleged comedies in a vain effort to make a light funster of Ralph Byrd, but neither *Broadway Big Shot* nor *Duke of the Navy* made 1942 a happy occasion for the newest indie company. The former had Byrd as a reporter who takes a prison sentence to work on an exposé from the inside and coaches the convict football eleven to a winning season, all done by the cast with apparently no conception of what comedy is, or how to play it. The Navy film had little maritime association and was mainly nonsense about a treasure hunt. Byrd had Veda Ann Borg and Sammy Cohen in the cast but they were unable to lend any help to a script dead set against everybody concerned, with Beaudine himself one of the three credited scenarists.

Mixed feelings were engendered by *Today I Hang*, which had Mona Barrie striving to prove Walter Wolf King innocent of a murder he didn't commit. Miss Barrie and King were accomplished performers, neither of whom had been seen on the screen too often. It was good to have them back, but the shallowness of their vehicle and its slipshod production made one ponder whether they shouldn't have waited for a more felicitous occasion. In the early scenes, before the crime, King would visit Miss Barrie and invariably enter her house through the side entrance — not out of furtiveness, but because the budget didn't call for any front door. The rest of the sets looked like rejects from a second-rate touring company. King appeared later in 1942 for PRC in *A Yank in Libya*, along with Joan Woodbury, H.B. Warner, Duncan Renaldo, comedian Parkyarkarkus and some of the most mildewed stock shots ever grafted on to new footage, grainy, spotted and barely legible, of native tribesmen, no doubt filmed during the dawn of cinema history.

Nor did Edith Fellows receive anything remotely approaching her abilities, especially after her charming performance in *Her First Romance* at Monogram. In *Girls' Town* she was again cast as an ugly duckling, sister of a beauty-contest winner (June Storey) who's trying to hit the Hollywood jackpot. The sister is curvaceous but snobbish, Fellows is plain but nice, and guess who lands the big movie contract? Nobody else cared, either. There were glimpses of former silent greats Alice White and Anna Q. Nilsson but the synthetic story negated everything else. Victor Halperin was a far piece from his "Zombie" films, and it proved to be his last film.

Other old-timers weren't faring so well at PRC. Neil Hamilton, who had been impressive in *Dangerous Lady*, had to impersonate a playboy in *Too Many Women*, and Hamilton was too mature for the role. Harry Langdon and Charles Rogers, who had teamed at Monogram, were seen

Sidney Blackmer (left), Byron Foulger, and Lynn Starr in a tense domestic scene from "The Panther's Claw."

in *House of Errors*, with Langdon writing the original story. It was a slapstick melange concerning new machine-gun inventions and a couple of dumb erstwhile reporters after the story. It wasn't a complete fiasco, with Langdon and Rogers indulging in some broad but amusing antics. But for those who remembered, it was pitiful to recall that Langdon once approached Chaplin in popularity.

PRC was finally getting around to the war news by the spring of 1942, and a spy thriller ready to be sent out as *Dawn Express* was hastily changed to *Nazi Spy Ring*. Another title failed to provide any improvement in the quality of the film, with Michael Whalen, Anne Nagel, Constance Worth and William Bakewell. *They Raid by Night* told of the commandos, with Lyle Talbot, June Duprez and Victor Varconi seemingly playing the entire thing in front of a process screen with grainy newsreel footage flashed on it to simulate exterior action. For her second and last for the company, Ann Corio was joined by Buster Crabbe to fight the Nazis in Africa in *Jungle Siren*, which was actually the best of the three, which should give some idea.

Alan Baxter (right) and Ernest Dorian as his oriental nemesis in "Prisoner of Japan."

Amid all the dross, PRC did manage some films of minor interest. Anthony Abbot's sleuth Thatcher Colt was revived in the person of Sidney Blackmer in *The Panther's Claw*. Martin Mooney did the screenplay with William Beaudine directing, and it turned out surprisingly well. Byron Foulger walked away with acting honors as a Milquetoast murder suspect, while Blackmer invested Colt with his usual authority. The mystery wasn't very mysterious, but the film was good enough to have merited a sequel and even a series, but no further ones were made. Beaudine and crew went to prison—figuratively—for *Men of San Quentin*, filmed entirely on location at the big house, giving the routine convict yarn an authenticity wanting in most films of similar background. Even the credit music was performed by the prison band. Another type of prison tale, in which a scientist (Alan Baxter) is held in captivity by a Japanese secret agent (Ernest Dorian) on a Pacific isle formed the basis of *Prisoner of Japan*, a strange and largely unsuccessful war drama produced by Seymour Nebenzal and directed and coscripted by Arthur Ripley. Overdone for the most part, with unrestrained and in a few cases overripe performances, Ripley's offbeat and sometimes bizarre direction made it worth watching. Ripley was a Sennett graduate and had been a comedy associate of Harry Langdon in the silent era, but his comedy background was buried for the dramatic endeavors, which often bordered on the macabre. Ripley's later work was sparse, but the few films he did make his forgotten career well worth examination. He spent his last days teaching at a university.

Anna May Wong appeared in two war films, vastly different in quality because of their directors. *Bombs Over Burma* was directed and partially written by Joseph H. Lewis, about skulduggery on the Burma Road. Lewis played the film in long stretches without dialogue, his camera telling the story pictorially; the final scene, of a German agent (Leslie Denison) meeting his death surrounded by Chinese guerrillas, was graphically constructed. The pictorial style used by Lewis made the film move at a snail's pace, but indications were that the former film editor had something to offer. Contrastingly, *Lady from Chungking* was directed by William Nigh without frills, or much care. Miss Wong was once again a Chinese patriot, and the cast featured Harold Huber as an enemy general, Mae Clarke as a White Russian, and Rick Vallin and Paul Bryar as Flying Tigers hiding out. Huber played the general the same way he did gangster roles, which was good, in a way.

A previous 1942 Nigh-directed drama, *City of Silent Men*, just missed being a sleeper. A story of ex-cons trying to go straight in a small town, Joseph Hoffman's script had realism, dialogue that didn't strain the ears, and plausible development for the most part. Nigh's direction staged it powerfully, and the cast of Frank Albertson, June Lang, Jan Wiley, Emmett Lynn and Dick Curtis gave praiseworthy performances. All the film needed was a bit more time carefully spent, and a bit more money.

Most of the remainder of 1942 PRC product dealt with gangsters, crime or whodunit puzzles, reliable standbys of indie companies catering to action and grind theater houses.

Baby Face Morgan played it for laughs, with Richard Cromwell as a rube posing as a tough racketeer. Robert Armstrong, Chick Chandler and Mary Carlisle lent strong support and while it never scaled any heights it was a passable spoof of the genre. *A Night for Crime* was murder in Hollywood and murder on the cast topped by Glenda Farrell and Lyle Talbot, chintzy production and lumbering pace mitigating against it. Joseph H. Lewis redeemed the schedule somewhat with his *Secrets of a Co-ed*, featuring Otto Kruger as a criminal lawyer put to the test when his daughter (Tina Thayer) becomes involved with a slimy racketeer (Rick Vallin). It had been done time out of number in the past and Lewis was unable to add anything but some camera angles, but these helped to a degree — it received favorable mention as a "good little picture" from a few Hollywood columnists. In *Tomorrow We Live*, it was Ricardo Cortez who played the slimy racketeer and Jean Parker the college girl in peril of his clutches. Bart Lytton wrote some pretentious flowery dialogue which Edgar G. Ulmer directed, but it didn't work. Seymour Nebenzal produced.

Boss of Big Town inveighed against food racketeers and deserved a look because it allowed John Litel to play the hero role, and even to finish the film by getting the girl (Florence Rice). Litel was always playing somebody's father, so it was heartening to see there was life in the old boy. Otherwise it told its tale without undue fuss and was pleasant. And in *The Payoff*, Lee Tracy ingratiatingly revived his fast-talking reporter characterization, giving the gangster story a lift, as did the welcome presences of Tom Brown, Evelyn Brent, Jack La Rue, Ian Keith and Robert Middlemass of the familiar-face brigade. Direction by Arthur Dreifuss had its moments, too.

Exceptions to the gangster-crime-whodunit PRC cycle were *Queen of Broadway*, a heart-tugger with Buster Crabbe, Rochelle Hudson and an orphan boy played by Donald Mayo, mix well and pour for sobs; *The Yanks Are Coming*, an execrable musical with an orchestra leader who couldn't act, Henry King, and some luckless individuals who shall be nameless; and *Miss V. from Moscow*.

Miss V. from Moscow featured Lola Lane as a Soviet agent in occupied Paris, confounding the Nazis and aiding a downed American flier (Howard Banks). It may well be one of the worst movies *ever made* by any standards; certainly the worst movie of its year.

PRC's next was *The Mad Monster* (1942), made in five days' time, with George Zucco as the dastardly scientist, western heavy Glenn Strange as the result of his experiments, Johnny Downs, Anne Nagel and Mae Busch. Zucco, a suave bulging-eyed English actor of considered ability and little good fortune in selecting his roles, became the company boogeyman.

Dead Men Walk was his first horror effort of 1943, and it was better than *The Mad Monster* because it was made in six days, by the same crew — the Sig Neufeld unit, with director Sam Newfield, writer Fred Myton, photographer Jack Greenhalgh, all departing from their western projects for the moment. Zucco was cast as twins, one of them a vampire back from the dead; Dwight Frye was happily on hand in much the same slavish manner as he was in the old *Dracula;* Mary Carlisle was the ingenue; and a pleasant-looking young man named Nedrick Young passed for the hero (Nedrick Young, later an award-winning writer for Stanley Kramer).

Horror of another kind was provided by Barton MacLane's *Man of Courage*, officially PRC's inaugural 1943 release. MacLane had a hand in writing the dialogue, so he had no one but himself to blame for the shocking ineptitudes, unless it would be producer Lester Cutler or director Alexis Thurn-Taxis. MacLane played a governor threatened by blackmail and along with everyone else involved, looked bad throughout.

Patsy Kelly starred in a couple of 1943 PRC comedies, *My Son, The Hero* and *Danger! Women at Work*, both nicely cast with capable players but neither of any special distinction. Comedy of a more subtle variety came from Arthur Ripley as a direct contrast to his grim *Prisoner of Japan*. This time Ripley produced, and Steve Sekely directed, *Behind Prison Walls*, reuniting Alan Baxter and Gertrude Michael from Ripley's previous film. Despite the title, it was a gentle, witty, somewhat intellectualized script by Van Norcross about a scheming tycoon (Tully Marshall) and his socialistic son (Baxter), both of whom go to prison and while there continue to finagle the stock market and outwit business rivals. An oddity from any company and a downright treasure coming from PRC, its soft-sell approach probably was the cause of its bypassing by most audiences, most of whom were in hopes of a prison yarn, with escaping cons and tough atmospherics. For those who saw it, it was a pleasant surprise. It was also the last film for the elderly Tully Marshall, best remembered from the silent *The Covered Wagon*.

A try for haunted-house humor, *The Ghost and the Guest*, didn't spark any hilarity even with Morey Amsterdam writing the script and James Dunn trying his best. William Nigh, again. George Zucco eschewed horror for straight suspense in *The Black Raven*, a sort of "Grand Hotel" with mayhem.

The big news from PRC for the first half of 1943 was its epic of the war, *Corregidor*, with Elissa Landi making a welcome return to the screen opposite Otto Kruger, and including a poem specially written for the film by Alfred Noyes (of "... the highwayman came riding, riding, riding...") and what was announced as a top-grade production budget. When finally viewed, the patron may have been pleased to see a tale of Doctor Landi in love with Doctor Donald Woods, and loved by Doctor Kruger, who knows she loves Doctor Woods, even though she tells Doctor Kruger that her love for Doctor Woods is no more, and so on for an hour and a quarter. The war was represented via a lot of newsreel footage of bombings and stock footage of explosions, and occasionally one of the characters would mention Bataan or Corregidor. That, plus one rather well-staged scene of hand-to-hand combat that assuredly never happened that way. In all, a messy production (by William Nigh). The war deserved better.

It didn't get much better with *Submarine Base*, with John Litel, Alan Baxter, Fifi D'Orsay, Eric Blore and Iris Adrian all stranded in a soggy tale of Nazi spies and subs off the coast of Brazil. Even Frank Buck chipped in to stop the Axis in *Tiger Fangs*, as he hustled to save the old rubber plantations. But he couldn't save the picture. Nor did Duncan Renaldo, nor did June Duprez, a talented actress from England who could have benfitted from some rescuing herself, since she had been getting poor scripts from PRC.

The company shot a wad on *Isle of Forgotten Sins*, but the expenditure failed to "show" properly on the screen. The remainder of 1943 was taken up with a succession of minor musicals and another Barton

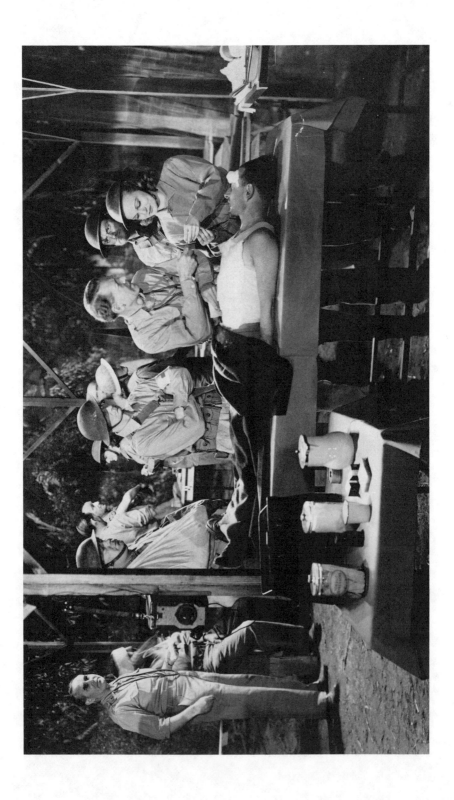

MacLane drama, *The Underdog*, a boy-and-dog idea of some merit, good direction from William Nigh, and a believable performance by young Bobby Larson. The musicals featured Armida, Rosemary Lane and Frances Langford at one time or another and were nondescript except for the casting of Veda Ann Borg and Edgar Kennedy in the Armida vehicle, and Miss Langford's stylish way with a tune.

The new year began promisingly for action and adventure fans with *Nabonga*, starring Buster Crabbe trekking through the PRC jungle growth in search of a "white witch" that turns out to be a lost girl, played by a fetching newcomer, Julie London. Villainy was taken care of by Barton MacLane and Fifi D'Orsay, and the encouraging thing was that it wasn't as ludicrous as it could have been. A few months later, Crabbe starred in a boxing drama with young Donald Mayo of *Queen of Broadway* repeating for the heart-tugs; *The Contender* had its moments, and a persuasive performance by Crabbe, with Sam Newfield offering one of his better directorial jobs.

Crabbe was capable, but he was obligated to the cowboy series for PRC. And where were the leading men going to come from in the war year of 1944? As the song lyric had it, the pickings were poor and the crop was lean—and when the perch was precariously on the bottom rung of the ladder, as was PRC's position, some finagling had to be indulged in to keep up the schedule. The first half of 1944 presented some interesting alternatives amidst the available manpower. *Men on Her Mind* was a true-confessions type of romance with Mary Beth Hughes. Her suitors were Edward Norris and Ted North, draft-resistant status, and Alan Edwards, a more mature type. *Lady in the Death House* top-billed Jean Parker, the innocent on death row for murder, with Lionel Atwill on the law's side for a change as a friendly psychologist, and what passed for the romantic lead was given to Douglas Fowley, a superb but typed actor, normally the perennial gangster in the casting directories.

The Monster Maker had J. Carrol Naish inflicting a distorting disease on Ralph Morgan, who was further victimized by unskilled makeup and looked like he was wearing rubber padding on his face, which was illegal during wartime shortages. Wanda McKay, playing Morgan's daughter, needed slight romantic interest and was so provided with Terry Frost, much more convincing as a western baddie.

Shake Hands with Murder featured the brassy Iris Adrian as a bail-bond broker, with Frank Jenks her partner and Douglas Fowley the innocent man in trouble. No romance. Terry Frost was given the assignment once more to clinch with the girl, Maris Wrixon in this instance, in *Waterfront*, with the main attention going to John Carradine and J. Carrol Naish as Nazi spies. Benny Fields, no youth at this stage, starred in

Opposite: Otto Kruger (operating surgeon, center) and Elissa Landi (right) fight the perils of "Corregidor."

June Carlson (left) and Fifi D'Orsay settle their differences in "Delinquent Daughters.

Minstrel Man with an enhanced PRC budget and smooth direction by Joseph H. Lewis, tuning up for his stint directing the musical numbers for *The Jolson Story* later. *Machine Gun Mama* starred Armida and featured Wallace Ford, who was in his late forties.

Delinquent Daughters concerned just what the title suggests. And *Seven Doors to Death* was a pleasing mystery top-billing Chick Chandler, who hadn't had a lead in years and who was, like Frank Jenks, recognized as a comedy second banana. So far as PRC was concerned, the films were being made, but the masculine representation was either a bit long in the tooth or nonmagnetic. At that, it was a refreshing change, for their leads placed emphasis upon talent rather than sex appeal, and in more than one case helped their little movie over some obstacles presented by scripts, production and directorial defects.

In the fall of 1944, inaugurating the 1944–45 season, PRC gave evidence that they were about to move upward. Two features released in close proximity rated with the best of the company's output to date, and would have been commendable coming from any source.

William K. Howard, having directed a mildly-received James Cagney film for Cagney's own company, came to PRC to guide a sentimental story by Frank Craven with a script by Milton Lazarus, *When the Lights Go On Again*. A song with that title was currently popular, and the plot of a returned war veteran suffering from fatigue and amnesia catered to topical interest. Although aimed directly at the heartstrings, under Howard it never became maudlin; and with so many of the men in uniform already on the way home, it had an extra amount of appeal. In the role of the mentally-disturbed vet, James Lydon, not too long ago Jimmy Lydon of the Henry Aldrich frappes, gave a sober, thoughtful performance that meant the beginning of the end of adolescent parts for him. He was ably supported by a carefully chosen cast of solid performers, among them Grant Mitchell, Regis Toomey, George Cleveland, Harry Shannon, Lucien Littlefield and Dorothy Peterson.

Bluebeard was exploited as a horror film and as such was successful. But it had several uncommon virtues for those not amenable to the genre, were they willing to give it a chance. Not based on the infamous career of Landru, as was Chaplin's later film, *Bluebeard* told of a puppeteer and artist whose mental quirks turn him into a periodic strangler of women. In the role, John Carradine gave what remains as one of his best, if not his absolute best, performance. His restraint under conditions that would tempt a Lugosi to overplay was remarkable, and he used his deep, rich voice, one of the best in films, to its fullest advantage. Jean Parker, a near-victim, Nils Asther, the law, and Ludwig Stossel, a conniving art dealer, gave Carradine competent backing, and Edgar Ulmer came through with an excellent job of direction, like Carradine's performance restrained and expertly conceived. The film's pictorial appearance is notable, getting the most from an adequate but still severely limited budget. Photographic credit is given to Jockey A. Feindel; below his name is a credit for "production design" to Eugen Schüfftan, one of Europe's most renowned cameramen, who was in this country at the time — and who didn't belong to the cameramen's union and therefore was unable to work. Or was he? In any event, Feindel had a reputation as one of the best camera operators in Hollywood, which is not quite the same as full photographer.

James Lydon teamed with Freddie Bartholomew, and Edward Everett Horton and Tom Tully, for a mild mistaken-identity comedy, *The Town Went Wild*, which Ralph Murphy came over from Paramount to direct. And brassy Iris Adrian gave way to brassy Robin Raymond to team with Frank Jenks in *Rogues Gallery*, patterned after but no sequel to *Shake Hands with Murder*. The latter ended PRC's 1944 output.

PRC clumped a trio of potential hits together in early 1945, hoping to make a box office killing, but only one possessed a worthy amount of quality, or novelty. *Strange Illusion* told of a boy (James Lydon) who believed his father to have been murdered most foully, and the scoundrel who accomplished the bloody deed (Warren William) was now paying court to his mother (Sally Eilers). Edgar G. Ulmer had the good sense not to stress the relationship to Shakespeare to the limit however, and the current trend in thrillers with a soupçon of psychoanalysis added interest to the modern-dress edition of the Bard. Boss-man of the company, Leon Fromkess, produced with extra care attendant, as he did with *Bluebeard* and *When the Lights Go On Again*.

"Out of the Night" (also known as "Strange Illusion") was directed by PRC's Edgar Ulmer.

Not so inviting was *Fog Island*, all about a search for loot on an isolated isle, with character actors George Zucco, Lionel Atwill, Veda Ann Borg, Jerome Cowan and others wading through the dullness, not alleviated by some cumbersome direction by Terry Morse. *Crime, Inc.* proved another disappointment, although given a better grade production and good cast including Leo Carrillo, Tom Neal, Sheldon Leonard, singer Martha Tilton in a laudable acting stint, Lionel Atwill and Harry Shannon. It was based on a story by Martin Mooney; Mooney was a former crime reporter who had faced a prison term for refusing to divulge information, and had parlayed this bit of gangland exotica into a career as a screen writer and producer. Neal played the approximation of the Mooney character and Lew Landers directed, but there was no sense of the gangster period which it was supposed to represent and the pace lagged considerably. As yet, crime shows were not ready for a renaissance and were still relegated to the minor theaters.

Much further down on the scale but better than the norm was *The Lady Confesses*, a whodunit played with style by Mary Beth Hughes, Hugh Beaumont and Edmund MacDonald, under Sam Newfield's direction. Another refugee from the range, Dave O'Brien, starred in *The Phantom of 42nd Street*, a backstage mystery with a nifty title and nothing else to back it up. O'Brien did much better when he forsook PRC and concentrated upon his pratfalls for Pete Smith at MGM.

PRC released an exploitation special in mid-1945, demurely titled *Why Girls Leave Home*. It told of illegal gambling and other hotcha stuff occurring at a questionable nitery, and the cast had some compatible types — Paul Guilfoyle, Elisha Cook, Jr., Lola Lane, Constance Worth, Thomas Jackson and Pamela Blake as the singer who is instrumental in blowing the whole sweet deal. The crusading reporter was personified by none other than Sheldon Leonard, who seemed aghast at playing a hero type and did his chore with accustomed relish. Insignificant though the film was, it was nominated for an Academy Award at the next session, for a ditty by Jerry Livingston and Ray Evans, "The Cat and the Canary."

A PRC release slated for fall 1945 was an original story by actor Sheldon Leonard called *Shadow of Terror*. It was about a research chemist (Richard Fraser) who has the formula for the most powerful explosive in the world, of how he was beset by spies in an attempt to wrest the formula from him, and of his eventual triumph. An average spy yarn, directed in average fashion by old faithful Lew Landers. While still in the cans awaiting final editing, a headline event occurred on August 6, 1945. The atom bomb was dropped on Hiroshima; by the first of September, the war was over and peace treaties were being signed in Tokyo Bay. The explosive formula was never mentioned in *Shadow of Terror*; PRC obtained newsreel clips of the atomic test explosions (just made public), tacked them onto the end of the film, had a narrator's voice intoning that

Pamela Blake (seated on piano) leads an impromptu swing session in "Why Girls Leave Home."

this was Fraser's secret all along, and the movie was ready for theaters by the first week in September. It was such a rush job that the atomic bomb footage had to be physically spliced in to the footage, rather than printed into the original negative. But PRC had made a coup. The war was over, and a "B" picture was there first.

PRC Westerns

by Les Adams, Buck Rainey,
and William K. Everson

PRC attracted a large number of surprisingly good western stars such as Tim McCoy, Buster Crabbe, Bob Livingston, and Bob Steele, and some lesser ones: George Houston, Tex Ritter, James Newill, Dave O'Brien, Bill Boyd (a radio singer, not the Hopalong Cassidy star), Lash La Rue, and Eddie Dean. While some of the first McCoy and Crabbe westerns were quite good, the studio's output as a whole was shoddy, their westerns fast but totally lacking in any kind of polish. The exploitation of Cinecolor gave some of their Eddie Deans a superficial edge over the others, but Dean was not popular and his films eventually reverted to black and white. A *New York Daily News* critic was not impressed by one of his later works and was moved to remark: "Eddie Dean's latest is in black and white rather than color, but the improvement is hardly noticeable; you can still see him."

PRC and Monogram seriously attempted to compete with Republic in the manufacture of low-budget westerns for the "B" market. PRC's product invariably was a shoddy one, the cheapness showing in every detail. Yet the pictures made money and were useful in filling the bottom half of a double feature "B" program when scheduled with a better quality western from Republic, Universal, Columbia, or Monogram in the top half.

Monogram's product was far superior to that of PRC in quality but, in general, did not measure up to that of Republic or the other majors. Some films, though, were exceptions, especially several in the Johnny Mack Brown and *Rough Riders* series.

PRC teamed singers Art Davis and Bill (Cowboy Rambler) Boyd with Lee Powell for a series in 1941–42. Powell was a competent performer and had potential as an actor, whereas Davis had potential as a personality on the basis of his voice and Autry-like charisma. Boyd, a Dallas, Texas, radio singer, had little going for him. After only six entries in the series it had to be discontinued when Davis and Powell entered the

35

military service. Powell was later killed in a Marine assault of a Japanese–held island in the South Pacific in August 1944.

The Buster Crabbe–Al St. John series was PRC's most popular one, in production between 1942–46. Although cheaply made, like all PRC features, these films were usually enjoyable. Crabbe and St. John made a good team and Charles King and Kermit Maynard were usually in the supporting lineup, which was a plus factor for discriminating buffs. Appeal was primarily to the rural and kiddie audience and bookings were usually restricted to second- and third-rate houses. Buster was simply not given a chance to rise above mediocrity in his PRC films. Credit is due to both Crabbe and St. John for their personal popularity when evaluating the success of their western series, for every aspect of production and story was poor. Suffice it to say that none of the films ever won an Academy Award for anything, or even an honorable mention. But they were horse operas, and their effulgence lay in the fact that Buster was tough and implacable, Al St. John was funny, the girls stayed pretty much out of the way, and the outlaws were familiar and predictable. Two of the better entries in the series were *His Brother's Ghost* (1945) in which St. John plays twin brothers, much to the consternation of Charlie King, and *Ghost of Hidden Valley* (1946), with a little different story twist.

The *Lone Rider* series was produced by PRC in 1942 with George Houston in the lead and in 1943 with Robert Livingston as star. The *Texas Rangers* series was in production until 1945 with Dave O'Brien, Jim Newill, and Guy Wilkerson comprising the trio that was supposed to compete with the Range Busters, the Three Mesquiteers, the Rough Riders, and the Trail Blazers in the trio market. Tex Ritter ultimately replaced Newill, in 1944, but it was O'Brien who carried the series throughout its twenty-one–film life span. The series was not a memorable one, but it did make money — a slight consideration of all concerned. Bob Steele's last series as a star was produced by PRC in 1945–46 and toward the end of 1945 Eddie Dean made his debut in *Song of Old Wyoming* opposite Jennifer Holt. Filmed in Cinecolor, the film introduced not only Dean (who had been around for years as a bit player) but also Al, soon to be Lash, La Rue. Dean's chief attribute was a good singing voice, but it was apparent that he would be no real threat to Autry or Rogers.

When PRC went out of business in 1948, Lash La Rue and Al St. John quickly found work for an outfit called Western Adventure Productions in a series produced by Ron Ormond and directed by Ray Taylor. Later the releases were credited to White-Houck and directed by Ron Ormond. *King of the Bullwhip* (1949) interestingly foreshadowed the hard times to come for "B" feature players in that six former stars played supporting roles in a cheapie western for union wages. Besides La Rue and St. John as costars, the film boasted Michael Whalen, Anne Gwynne, Jack Holt, Tom Neal, Dennis Moore, and George J. Lewis — $50,000 worth of talent for probably $1,000.

Lash La Rue was a whip-cracking, obstreperous, black-garbed, sulky, gangster-looking, tough-talking poor physical specimen who never should have been cast as a lead. His success was a quirk. He was so unbelievably bad as an actor that people were drawn to him either in sympathy or in disbelief that such a cowboy could be filling the screen once occupied by Buck Jones, Ken Maynard, and George O'Brien. Perhaps audiences came to see the outrageously funny buffoon that shuffled and fumbled his way through each film and who shared costarring honors — Al St. John, a bewhiskered, lovable, scene-stealing little guy who was consistently picking fights for his partner to finish. St. John, a holdover from the Keystone Kops days when he starred in numerous two-reelers, became one of western filmdom's most popular sidekicks in spite of almost exclusive work in the cheapies of PRC and similar independents. As "Fuzzy Q. Jones" he found a place in the hearts of "B" devotees and stayed there.

PRC Corporate Structure

PRC Pictures, Inc.
Subsidiary of Pathé Laboratories, Inc.
625 Madison Avenue, New York, NY 10022
PL3-6100
(Producer-Distributor)

Officers
Exec. V-P in chg of Production: Leon Fromkess
In chg of Domestic Sales: Leo J. McCarthy
Treasurer: Joseph H. Lamm

Department Heads
Exchange Operations: Armand Schneck
Mgr. Foreign Department: Roberto D. Socas
Eastern Dir. Advt.-Pub.: Samuel S. Kestenbaum
Contract Dept.: John Consentino
Print Dept.: Janet Rosenthal
Accounting Dept.: David P. Wiener
Super. Advertising-Publicity: Martin Mooney
West Coast Dir. Advt.-Pub.: Joseph O'Sullivan
Asst. to Leon Fromkess and Studio Operations: Ben Schwalb
Production Manager: Chris Beute

Production Affiliates
Constance Bennett Productions, Sig Neufeld Productions, Alexander-
    Stern Productions, American Productions, Jack Schwarz Productions.

PRC Productions, Inc.
7324 Santa Monica Blvd.
Los Angeles 46, CA
Hillside 8111

and

Robert Armstrong (being restrained) is in tough company in "Arson Squad."

PRC Pictures, Inc.
625 Madison Avenue
New York, NY 10022
PL3-6100

    Leon Fromkess, in July 1944, was elected president of PRC Pictures, Inc., officially assuming the post he had held for all practical purposes since the resignation of O. Henry Briggs, some months before.

1944–45 PRC Structure

PRC Pictures, Inc.
625 Madison Avenue, New York, NY 10022
PL3-6100
7324 Santa Monica Boulevard, Hollywood 46, California
(PRC Productions); subsidiary of Pathé Industries, Inc.
Chairman of the Board: Kenneth M. Young
President and Head of Production: Leon Fromkess
Board of Directors: Leon Fromkess, Kenneth M. Young, Raymond J. Morfa, Allen Kirby, Robert Young, Henry J. Guild, J. Stimson Young, Robert W. Purcell
Home Office Operations: George Fleitman

Director, Publicity & Advertising: Don McElwaine
East Coast Publicity: Arnold Stoltz
Manager, Control Department: John Consentino
Manager, Foreign Department: Roberto D. Socas
Asst. Mgr., Foreign Department: M. Vargas
Print Department: Janet Rosenthal
Accounting Department: Sol Citrin, Superintendent, Home Accounts;
   William Kline, Superintendent, Branch Accounts

Production Affiliates
Alexander Stern Productions; Green-Rouse; Jack Schwarz Productions;
   Sigmund Neufeld (all at 7324 Santa Monica Boulevard, Hollywood 46,
   California).

Date and Place of Incorporation
Producers Releasing Corporation of America, 1940, New York;
   reorganized as PRC Pictures, Inc., 1944, Ohio.

Distribution
General Sales Manager: Harry Thomas
Eastern Division Sales Manager: Sidney Kulick
Southern Division Sales Manager: Fred A. Rohrs
Western Division Sales Manager: Jack K. Adams, Jr.

Branches
Buffalo: Jack Berkson, franchise; Leo Murphy, manager, 505 Pearl
   Street.
Atlanta: Ike Katz, franchise and manager, 163 Walton St., NW.
Boston: Harry A. Goldman; franchise and manager, 12 Piedmont Street.
Charlotte: Ike Katz, franchise and manager; 224 West Second Street.
Chicago: Henri Elman, franchise; 1327 South Wabash Avenue; Morton
   Van Praag, manager.
Cincinnati: PRC Exchange of Cincinnati, Inc., 1632 Central Parkway;
   Harry Bugie, branch manager.
Cleveland: PRC Exchange of Cleveland, Inc., Film Exchange Building,
   2112 Payne Avenue; Mark Goldman, branch manager.
Dallas: PRC Exchange of Dallas, Inc., Film Exchange Building; Jack K.
   Adams, Jr., acting branch manager.
Denver: J.H. Ashby, franchise; J.J. Ashby, manager, 2071 Broadway.
Detroit: PRC Exchange of Detroit, Inc., 2310 Cass Avenue; William Fle-
   mion, branch manager.
Indianapolis: Joseph W. Bohn, franchise; Sam H. Abrams, manager; 438
   North Illinois Street.
Kansas City, MO: R.H. Patt, John Muchmore, franchise; B. Miller,
   manager; 1717 Wyandotte Street.

Little Rock: B.F. Busby, franchise and manager; 106-8 South Cross Street.

Los Angeles: PRC Exchange of Los Angeles, Inc., 1966 South Vermont Avenue; Harry Stern, branch manager.

Milwaukee: Joe Strother, franchise; Ben Marcus, manager; 641 North Seventh Street.

Minneapolis: Abbott M. Swartz, franchise; 1109 Currie Avenue.

New Orleans: P.A. Sliman, franchise and manager; 221 South Liberty Street.

New York: Bert Kulick, franchise; Francis Kulick, manager; 630 Ninth Avenue.

Oklahoma City: E.L. Walker and Harry McKannas, franchise; 9½ North Lee Street.

Omaha: PRC Pictures, Film Exchange Building; Harry Rogers, Manager.

Philadelphia: Herbert Given, franchise and manager; 1321 Vine Street.

Pittsburgh: PRC Exchange of Pittsburgh, Inc., 415 Van Braam Street; Lew Lefton, branch manager.

Portland, OR: See Seattle.

Salt Lake City: J.H. Ashby, franchise; A.G. Edwards, manager; 252 East First South Street.

St. Louis: Andy Dietz, franchise; 3206 Olive Street.

San Francisco: Sam Sobel, franchise; Armand Cohn, manager; 247 Golden Gate Avenue.

Seattle: Lloyd Lamb, franchise and manager; 2321 Second Avenue.

Washington, DC: George Gill, franchise and manager; 203 Eye Street, NW.

Canada: PRC, Ltd. (H.J. Allen, pres. and gen. manager; Nat Taylor, secy-treas.), 227 Victoria Street, Toronto.

Near East Distributors: United States Film Co. (subsidiary of Sodeco Trading Corporation), 233 Broadway, New York, NY 10007.

The title "Dawn Express" was changed to "Nazi Spy Ring" to capitalize on war news of 1942.

PRC War Roster

Enlisted men from PRC Pictures — December 1943: George Batcheller, Jr., Ralph Bettenison, Capt. Edward Granneman, William Raynor, Jack Greenhalgh, Stanley Neufeld, Lt. Robert S. Benjamin, Lt. Com. Bert Kulick.

Edgar G. Ulmer's Wartime Propaganda Production

The Raphael G. Wolff organization showed great growth during 1943 and produced films for General Electric, Thompson Products, Cleveland, and the Ternstedt Division of General Motors. For General Electric, Wolff made subjects giving instruction in atomic-hydrogen arc-welding and also made Spanish versions of eight of these subjects for South America. He also produced four single-reel Kodachrome films for Coca-Cola, using 16mm film. Edgar Ulmer, PRC director, handled the direction on the four subjects.

Brief Biographies of Key PRC Personnel

Alexander, Max. Producer. **Pictures include:** In 1938: with Arthur Alexander produced *International Crime*, (GN). In 1941: produced *City of Missing Girls*. In 1942: *Swamp Woman, Today I Hang*. In 1944: *Seven Doors to Death, I Accuse My Parents*.

Beaudine, William. Director. Born New York City, Jan. 15, 1890. Became associated with motion pictures in 1904; then joined Biograph (1904–14); Kalem (1914–16); Universal (1916–17); Triangle (1917–18); Christie (1918–22); Goldwyn (1922–23); Warner Bros. (1923–27); Universal (1927); and First National (1928). **Pictures (since sound) include:** *Her Bodyguard, Two Hearts in Harmony, Misbehaving Husbands, Desperate Cargo, The Panther's Claw, One Thrilling Night, Phantom Killer, Foreign Agent, Prison Girls, The Ape Man, Hot Rhythm, Oh, What a Night, Leave It to the Irish, Adventures of Kitty O'Day, Bowery Champs, Crazy Knights, Swingin' on a Rainbow, Fashion Model, Come Out Fighting, Blonde Ransom*. Died 1970.

Cabanne, Christy. Director. Born St. Louis, MO, 1888; educated at St. Rose Academy, Culver Military Academy, Annapolis Naval Academy. Early career was spent in the Navy. Theatrical experience started in 1908. Entered pictures in 1910; directed Douglas Fairbanks, joined Fine Arts; assistant to D.W. Griffith; author, originally produced Metro serial; then organized own company; subsequently directed for Goldwyn, FBO, Associated Exhibitors, MGM, Tiffany-Stahl, Demille-Pathé, Columbia, RKO. **Pictures (from 1930) include:** *Annapolis, The Girl of the Limberlost, The Keeper of the Bees, We Who Are About to Die, Don't Tell the Wife, The Outcasts of Poker Flat, Annapolis Salute* (original director), various *Scattergood Baines* pictures (RKO), *Alias the Deacon, Drums of the Congo, Timber, Keep 'Em Slugging* (Universal). Died 1950.

Clifton, Elmer. Director, writer. Born Chicago, IL. Began as actor; on stage (Belasco stock company), on screen in early D.W. Griffith

44

pictures. First production as director: *Her Official Father* (Fine Arts). Associate director: *Way Down East* (Griffith); producer, screenplay writer, director: *Down to the Sea in Ships*; director, screenplay writer: *Six Cylinder Love, Warrens of Virginia, Swamp Woman*, etc. Produced talking-picture travelogue made on trip around world (*Vagabond Adventure Pictures*). Directed number of westerns starring Buck Jones. **Pictures include:** *Sundown Kid, Old Chisholm Trail, Seven Doors to Death* (screenplay & director), *Spook Town, Whispering Skull*. Died 1949.

Clifton, Leon E. Publicist. Born Baltimore, MD, July 12, 1895; educated at University of Western Ontario, B.A. Began as journalist (variously reporter, editor, columnist); lecturer, radio writer, newspaper publisher; American representative for Haile Selassie, emperor of Ethiopia. In 1944 joined publicity department of PRC Pictures, Inc.

Cook, Elisha, Jr. Actor. Born San Francisco, December 26, 1907; educated at St. Albans, a Chicago boarding school. Joined Frank Bacon in *Lightnin'*, at the age of 14. Appeared with Ethel Barrymore in *Kingdom of God*, in *Henry, Behave, Many a Slip, Three Cornered Moon*, in London in *Coquette*. Played in vaudeville and summer stock companies. Appeared in *Chrysalis*, then *Ah, Wilderness*. Theatre Guild success. Signed by Paramount. **Pictures include:** *Two in a Crowd* (Universal); *Pigskin Parade* (20th–Fox). In 1937: *Love Is News, Wife, Doctor and Nurse, Danger — Love at Work, Life Begins in College* (20th–Fox); *Breezing Home* (Universal); *They Won't Forget* (Warner Bros.); *The Devil Is Driving* (Columbia). In 1938: *My Lucky Star, Submarine Patrol* (20th–Fox). In 1939: *Grand Jury Secrets* (Paramount). In 1940: *He Married His Wife, Tin Pan Alley* (20th–Fox); *Stranger on the Third Floor* (RKO). In 1942: *Sleepytime Gal* (Republic); *A-Haunting We Will Go, Manila Calling* (20th–Fox); *Wildcat* (Paramount). In 1944: *Up in Arms* (RKO), *Casanova Brown* (International Pictures); *Dark Waters* (United Artists); *Dark Mountain* (Paramount). In 1945: *Dillinger* (Monogram); *Why Girls Leave Home* (PRC). In 1946: *Cinderella Jones* (Warner Bros.).

Eilers, Sally. Actress. Born New York City, December 11, 1908. Dancer, on dramatic stage. Began screen career in Mack Sennett's *Goodbye Kiss;* later featured in many silent productions. **Pictures (since sound) include:** *Cradle Snatchers, Hat Check Girl, Three on a Honeymoon, Alias Mary Dow, Strike Me Pink, Everybody's Doing It, Lady Behave!, Full Confession, I Was a Prisoner on Devil's Island, A Wave, a Wac, a Marine, Strange Illusion*. Died 1978.

Fromkess, Leon. President PRC Pictures, Inc., and general manager PRC Studios, PRC Productions, PRC Exchanges. Born New York City,

Lobby cards from "Out of the Night" ("Strange Illusion"). Top: Sally Eilers and Warren William discuss their impending marriage. Bottom: Well, maybe not (Jayne Hazard, center).

November 23, 1901; educated at Columbia University. Did original Wall Street financing for Columbia Pictures Corp., 1929. Joined Monogram January 1938, as treasurer. Resigned to join PRC as vice-president and general manager in charge of production. Member: Picture Pioneers. **Pictures include:** *Strange Illusion, Fog Island, When the Lights Go On Again, Bluebeard, Delinquent Daughters, Crime, Inc., The Great Mike, Minstrel Man, Hollywood and Vine, The Missing Corpse.* Died 1977.

Herman, Al. Director. Real name: Adam H. Foelker. Born Troy, NY, Feb. 22, 1887; educated at Troy and Manhattan Agricultural College. Entered motion picture industry 1913. **Pictures include:** *Starlight Over Texas, Where the Buffalo Roam, Song of the Buckaroo, Roll Wagons Roll, Rhythm of the Rio Grande, Pals of the Silver Sage, The Golden Trail, Arizona Frontier, Take Me Back to Oklahoma, The Pioneers, Gentleman from Dixie, Nazi Spy Ring, A Yank in Libya, Rangers Take Over, Miss V from Moscow, Shake Hands with Murder; Delinquent Daughters* (coproducer), *Rogue's Gallery, The Phantom of 42nd Street, The Missing Corpse.* Died 1967.

Judge, Arline. Actress. Born Bridgeport, CT, Feb. 21, 1912; educated at Ursuline Academy. In musicals and revues (*The Second Little Show, Silver Slipper,* etc.). **Pictures include:** *Are These Our Children?, Girl Crazy, Age of Consent, Looking for Trouble, Shoot the Works, Name the Woman, Law of the Jungle, Girls in Chains, McGuerins from Brooklyn, Song of Texas, Take It Big, The Contender, G.I. Honeymoon, From This Day Forward, Mad Wednesday.* Died 1974.

La Rue, Jack. Actor. Born New York City, 1902. Originally a piano tuner. On stage in *Crime, Diamond Lil, Fiesta* and others. **Pictures include:** In 1933: *The Story of Temple Drake, The Woman Accused, Terror Aboard, Girl in 419, Gambling Ship, To the Last Man* (Paramount); *Headline Shooter, Radio, The Kennel Murder Case* (Warner Bros.). In 1934: *Miss Fane's Baby Is Stolen, Good Dame* (Paramount); *Take the Stand, No Ransom* (Liberty). From 1935 in many pictures for major companies. In 1940: *Charlie Chan in Panama* (20th–Fox); *Forgotten Girls* (Republic); *Enemy Agent* (Universal); *Fugitive from a Prison Camp* (Columbia); *East of the River* (Warner Bros.). In 1941: *Paper Bullets, Hard Guy* (PRC); *Ringside Maisie* (MGM); *Gentleman from Dixie* (Monogram). In 1942: *Swamp Woman* (PRC); *Highways by Night* (RKO); *X Marks the Spot* (Republic). In 1943: *You Can't Beat the Law* (Monogram). Died 1984.

Lydon, Jimmy. Actor. Born Harrington Park, NJ, May 30, 1923; educated at St. Johns Military School. On New York stage (*Prologue to Glory, Sing Out the News,* etc.). On screen 1939 *Back Door to Heaven.*

Jimmy Lydon is comforted by Jayne Hazard in "Out of the Night" ("Strange Illusion").

Later pictures include: *The Thoroughbreds, Naval Academy,* various Henry Aldrich productions, *Out of the Night (Strange Illusion.)*

Mooney, Martin. Writer. Born New York City, April 17, 1896. Journalist, press agent, ghost writer; columnist, *N.Y. American,* etc.; playwright (*The Town's Woman, Sisters of the Chorus, The Ghost Writer*). From 1943 directed advertising and publicity, PRC Productions. Began screen writing 1935 with *Special Agent.* Since then, author of original stories, screenplays, continuities, etc. **Pictures include:** *Bullets or Ballots, Parole, Missing Girls, You Can't Buy Luck, Inside Information, Convicted Woman, Millionaires in Prison, Broadway Big Shot, The Panther's Claw.* From 1941 also produced *Men of San Quentin, Foreign Agent, Silent Witness, The Great Mike* (original story and associate producer); *Bluebeard* (associate producer); *Crime Inc.* (original story and associate producer); *Waterfront* (original story and collaborated on screenplay); *Minstrel Man* (collaborated on original story). Died 1967.

Neal, Tom. Actor. Born Evanston, IL, Jan. 28, 1914; educated at

Northwestern University, B.A., 1934; Harvard University, LL.B., 1938. On New York stage (*If This Be Treason, Love Is Not Simple, Spring Dance, June Night,* etc.). Screen debut 1938 in *Out West with the Hardys.* **Pictures include:** *Burn 'Em Up O'Connor, Another Thin Man, Within the Law, Flying Tigers, China Girl, Behind the Rising Sun, Good Luck Mr. Yates, The Racket Man, Two-Man Submarine, The Unknown, Thoroughbreds, Crime Inc., Unwritten Code.* Died 1972.

Neufeld, Sigmund. President, Sigmund Neufeld Productions, Inc.; formerly production executive, Producers Releasing Corporation. Born New York City, May 3, 1896; mother Mrs. Josephine Neufeld. In 1914–31: Universal Studios. In 1931: independent producer. **Pictures include:** In 1940: *Frontier Crusader, I Take This Oath, Mercy Plane* (Producers Releasing Corp.). In 1941: *Outlaws of the Rio Grande, Billy the Kid's Fighting Pals, The Lone Rider in Ghost Town, Billy the Kid in Santa Fe, Billy the Kid Wanted, The Lone Rider Fights Back, The Lone Rider Ambushed, Billy the Kid's Round-up* (PRC). In 1942: produced *Billy the Kid Trapped, Billy the Kid's Smoking Guns, Law and Order, Jungle Siren* (PRC). In 1943: *Overland Stagecoach, Mysterious Rider, Outlaws of Boulder Pass, Frontier Marshal in Prairie Pals, Fugitive of the Plains, Lone Rider in Wild Horse Rustlers, The Kid Rides Again* (PRC).

Newfield, Sam. Director. Born New York City, December 6, 1899. Entered motion picture industry in 1919; directed *The Excuse Makers, What Happened to Jane, Let George Do It* series. Buster Brown comedies and series of Arthur Lake comedies for Universal, last four of which were *French Leave, Horse Sense, Love-Birds, Hey Doctor;* and *His Maiden Voyage* for Universal. **Pictures include:** In 1933: *The Important Witness, Reform Girl,* (Tower); *Big Time or Bust* (State Rights); *Under Secret Orders* (Progressive). In 1934: *Marrying Widows, Beggar's Holiday* (Tower). In 1935: *Northern Frontier, Timber* (Ambassador); *Racing Luck* (Republic). In 1936: *Roaring Lead* (Republic); *Aces and Eights, Ghost Patrol* (Puritan); *Trail's End* (MLB); *Border Caballero* (Puritan). In 1937: *Melody of the Plains* (Spectrum); *Harlem on the Prairie* (Associated Features); *Colorado Kid* (Republic). In 1938: *Paroled to Die* (Republic); *The Rangers Roundup* (Spectrum); *Knight of the Plains* (Spectrum–Stan Laurel); *The Terror of Tiny Town* (Principal); *Frontier Scout* (Fine Arts–GN). In 1939: *Trigger Pals, Six Gun Rhythm* (GN). In 1940: *Secrets of a Model* (Continental). In 1941: *The Lone Rider in Ghost Town, The Lone Rider Ambushed, The Lone Rider Fights Back* (PRC). In 1943: *Danger! Women at Work, Tiger Fangs, Harvest Melody, The Black Raven, Wild Horse Rustlers, Western Cyclone, Death Rides the Plains, The Renegades, Blazing Frontier.* In 1944: *Wolves of the Range.* In 1945: *Raiders of Red Gap, His Brother's Ghost, Shadows of Death, Apology for Murder.* In 1946: *The Flying Serpent* (all PRC). Died 1964.

Dave O'Brien (right) and Kay Aldridge (left) seem less than impressed by Walter Catlett in this lobby-card still from "The Man Who Walked Alone."

Nigh, William. Director. Born Berlin, WI, Oct. 12, 1881; educated at California University. Entered motion picture industry 1911. Pictures include: *Mr. Wu, Four Walls, Lord Byron of Broadway, Men Are Such Fools, Mystery Liner, His Night Out, Crash Donovan, North of Nome, Atlantic Flight, Rose of the Rio Grande, Romance of the Limberlost, Streets of New York, Mutiny in the Big House, The Kid from Kansas, Mob Town, Mr. Wise Guy, Black Dragons, The Strange Case of Dr. Rx, Escape from Hong Kong, Secret Evidence, The Lady from Chungking, Tough As They Come, City of Silent Men, Corregidor, Where Are Your Children?, The Ghost and the Guest, The Underdog, Trocadero, Are These Our Parents?, They Shall Have Faith, Divorce.* Died 1955.

O'Brien, Dave. Actor. Born May 31, 1912, Big Springs, Texas. Pictures include: In 1933: *Jenny Gerhardt* (Paramount). In 1934: *Little Colonel* (20th–Fox). In 1935: *Welcome Home* (20th–Fox). In 1941: *Renfrew Mounted Police* series. In 1942: seven Pete Smith shorts (MGM); *Devil Bat* (PRC). In 1943: *Texas Ranger* western series, PRC. In 1944: *Tahiti Nights* (Columbia). In 1945: *The Phantom of 42nd Street* (PRC). Died 1969.

Savage, Ann. Actress. Real name Bernie Lyon. Born Columbia, SC, Feb. 19, 1921; educated at Max Reinhardt School of Dramatic Art,

Hollywood, CA. On stage in *Golden Boy*. On screen 1943 in *After Midnight with Boston Blackie*. **Pictures include:** *One Dangerous Night, More the Merrier, Two Senoritas from Chicago, Boston Blackie, What a Woman, Dangerous Blondes, Klondike Kate, Two-Man Submarine, The Unknown, Ever Since Eve, Between Us Girls, Dancing in Manhattan, Unwritten Code, Detour*.

Schwarz, Jack. Producer. In 1942: coproducer, *Girls Town;* producer, *Baby Face Morgan, Boss of Big Town* (PRC). In September 1942: signed by Producers Releasing Corp. with Lee Tracy as producer to make a series of topical newspaperman stories: first was *The Payoff*. A former exhibitor. **Pictures include:** *The Lady in the Death House, Sometimes I'm Happy, Enchanted Forest, Mexican Fiesta, Dixie Jamboree, Machine Gun Mama*.

Tannura, Philip. Cinematographer. Born New York City. In 1909 child player on stage; afterward, still photographer and cameraman Thomas A. Edison, Inc. Photographer for U.S. Signal Corps, World War I. Joined Paramount Eastern Studio; cameraman, Charles Ray Prod., FBO in Hollywood; joined Pathé and sent to France. Later opened London studio for Paramount; joined London Films. Cameraman for various Gaumont British and other British productions 1934–42; thereafter many in Hollywood, for PRC.

Toomey, Regis. Actor. Born Pittsburgh, PA, August 13, 1902; educated at University of Pittsburgh, received stage training at Carnegie Institute of Technology; married J. Kathryn Scott. Five years on stage New York and London. On the screen in 1929 in *The Wheel of Life, Illusion* (Paramount and others); from 1930 in many productions principal Hollywood producers. **Pictures include:** In 1942: *Bullet Scars, I Was Framed* (Warner Bros.); *The Forest Rangers* (Paramount); *Tennessee Johnson* (MGM). In 1944: *Follow the Boys, Phantom Lady* (Universal); *Song of the Open Road* (UA–Warner Bros.); *Dark Mountain* (Paramount); *Murder in the Blue Room* (Universal); *The Doughgirls* (Warner Bros.). Many PRC films.

Tracy, Lee. Actor. Real name William Lee Tracy. Born Atlanta, GA, April 14, 1898; educated at Western Military Academy, Alton, IL, Union College, Schenectady, NY. Stage, stock companies five years, road companies two years. New York plays include *The Show Off, Book of Charm, Wisdom Tooth, Broadway, The Front Page*. Screen debut 1930. **Pictures include:** *Big Time, On the Level, Born Reckless, Blessed Event, Washington Merry Go Round, Clear All Wires, Private Jones, Dinner at Eight, Turn Back the Clock, Bombshell, Advice to the Lovelorn, I'll Tell the World, Carnival, Two Fisted, Sutter's Gold, Criminal Lawyer,*

Warren William (left) confronts Jimmy Lydon in this staged publicity shot from "Out of the Night" ("Strange Illusion"). Mary McLeod, player, and Jayne Hazard look on.

Behind the Headlines, The Spellbinder, Millionaires in Prison, The Payoff. Died 1968.

Ulmer, Edgar George. Director, writer. Born Vienna, Austria, Sept. 17, 1900; educated at Academy of Arts & Sciences, Vienna; University of Belin, M.Ph. Assistant stage designer, Vienna; also actor; art director 1918, Decla-Bioscope Co. Joined Max Rheinhardt as assistant stage director and scene designer. In 1922 assistant and art director, F.W. Murnau (*The Last Laugh, Faust*). To U.S. 1923 with Rheinhardt; signed by Martin Beck; then to Universal as art director. Producer assistant 1926, Fox Films (*Four Devils, Sunrise, Our Daily Bread, Tabu*). Returned to Germany 1929, director and producer. In 1930 to Hollywood, unit art director, MGM; with Philadelphia Grand Opera Co., 1931. Then director of many pictures for independent producers. Member: Academy of Motion Picture Arts & Sciences; American Society of Acoustics; Dascho (Berlin). **Pictures include:** *The Black Cat, Damaged Lives, Natalka Poltevka, Green Fields, The Singing Blacksmith, Tomorrow We Live, Girls in Chains, Bluebeard, Strange Illusion.* Also writer (original story *Prisoner of Japan;* collaborated original screenplay *Corregidor*). Died 1972.

William, Warren. Actor. Real name Warren Krech. Born Aitkin, MN., 1895. On New York stage; entering pictures variously starred and featured many productions for Warner Bros. and later only Hollywood producers. In 1942: *Counter Espionage* (Columbia); *Eyes of the Underworld* (Universal). In 1943: *One Dangerous Night* (Columbia). In 1945: *Strange Illusion* (PRC). Died 1948.

Wisbar, Frank. Writer. Born Tilsit, Germany, Dec. 9, 1899. Playwright, publisher, editor in Germany, 1925–29. Producer UFA (*Maedchen in Uniform*, ect.), 1930–38. Lecturer on films, University of Berlin, Hamburg, Leipsig, Freiberg, 1935–38. Joined Minoco Films, New York 1942. Author of story for Monogram production *Woman in Bondage*. Pictures include: In 1945: *Strangler of the Swamp*. In 1946: *Devil Bat's Daughter, Lighthouse, Secrets of a Soroity Girl* (PRC). Died 1967.

Yarbrough, Jean. Director and producer. Born Marianna, AR, Aug. 22, 1900; educated at University of the South, Sewanee, TN. Entered motion picture industry as property man in 1922 with Hal Roach, then assistant director and director. Pictures include: *Top Sergeant Mulligan, Let's Go Collegiate, King of the Zombies, The Gang's All Here, Father Steps Out, The Devil Bat, Caught in the Act, South of Panama, Man from Headquarters, Law of the Jungle, So's Your Aunt Emma, She's in the Army, Police Bullets; Good Morning, Judge; Follow the Band, The Brute Man, Moon Over Las Vegas, Hi Ya Sailor, Let Yourself Go* (producer-director); *Twilight on the Prairie, Weekend Pass, So's Your Uncle, Get Going, In Society, Under Western Skies, Here Come the Co-eds* (director). Died 1975.

Zucco, George. Actor. Born Manchester, England, Jan. 11, 1886. On stage from 1908 (debut in Canada); in various prominent dramatic plays New York. First screen role recreating stage part in *Autumn Crocus*, Associated Talking Pictures. Followed roles in many Hollywood pictures including *Parnell, Cat and the Canary, Adventures of Sherlock Holmes, Hunchback of Notre Dame, International Lady*. In 1942: *My Favorite Blonde* (Paramount); *Halway to Shanghai, The Mummy's Tomb* (Universal); *The Black Swan, Dr. Renault's Secret* (20th–Fox). In 1943: *Black Raven, Dead Men Walk* (PRC); *Sherlock Holmes in Washington* (Universal). In 1944: *One Body Too Many* (Paramount); *The Seventh Cross* (MGM); *Shadows in the Night* (Columbia).

Filmographies of
Principal PRC Directors

Christy Cabanne
(William Christy Cabanne,
1888–1950)

Alias the Deacon (Universal, 1940)
Annapolis Salute (RKO, 1937. Also story)
Another Face (RKO, 1935)
Asalto sobre el chaco (Spanish version of *Storm over the Andes*) (Universal, 1935)
Behind the Green Lights (Mascot, 1935)
Black Diamonds (Universal, 1940)
Black Trail (Monogram, 1948)
Carne de cabaret (Spanish version of *Ten Cents a Dance*) (Columbia, 1931)
Cinderella Swings It (RKO, 1943)
Conspiracy (RKO, 1930)
Convicted (Artclass, 1931)
Criminal Lawyer (RKO, 1937)
Danger on Wheels (Universal, 1940)
Daring Daughters (Capitol, 1933)
The Dawn Trail (Columbia, 1930)
The Devil's Pipeline (Universal, 1940)
Dixie Jamboree (PRC, 1945)
Don't Tell the Wife (RKO, 1937)
Drums of the Congo (Universal, 1942)
The Eleventh Commandment (Alliance, 1933)
Everybody's Doing It (RKO, 1938)
A Girl of the Limberlost (Monogram, 1934)
Graft (Universal, 1931)

Hearts of Humanity (Majestic, 1932)
Hot Steel (Universal, 1940)
Hotel Continental (Tiffany, 1932)
Jane Eyre (Monogram, 1934)
Keep 'Em Slugging (Universal, 1943)
The Keeper of the Bees (Monogram, 1935)
King of the Bandits (Monogram, 1935)
The Last Outlaw (RKO, 1936)
Legion of Lost Flyers (Universal, 1938)
Man from Montreal (Universal, 1940)
The Man Who Walked Alone (PRC, 1945. Also associate producer, story)
Midnight Patrol (Monogram, 1932)
Midshipman Jack (RKO, 1933)
Money Means Nothing (Monogram, 1934)
The Mummy's Hand (Universal, 1940)
Mutiny on the Blackhawk (Universal, 1939)
Night Spot (RKO, 1938)
One Frightened Night (Monogram, 1935)
The Outcasts of Poker Flat (RKO, 1937)
Red-Haired Alibi (Tower, 1932)
Rendezvous at Midnight (Universal, 1935)
Restless Youth (Columbia, 1929)
Robin Hood of Monterey (Monogram, 1947. Also story)
Scared to Death (Golden Gate, 1946)
Scattergood Baines (RKO, 1941)

Scattergood Meets Broadway (RKO, 1941)
Scattergood Pulls the Strings (RKO, 1941)
Scattergood Rides High (RKO, 1942)
Scattergood Survives a Murder (RKO, 1942)
Sensation Hunters (Monogram, 1945)
Silver Trails (Monogram, 1948)
Sky Raiders (Columbia, 1931)
Smashing the Spy Ring (Columbia, 1938)
Storm over the Andes (Universal, 1935)
This Marriage Business (RKO, 1938)
Timber (Universal, 1942)
Top Sergeant (Universal, 1942)
Tropic Fury (Universal, 1939)
The Unwritten Law (Majestic, 1932)
We Who Are About to Die (RKO, 1936)
Western Limited (Monogram, 1932)
The Westland Case (Universal, 1937)
When Strangers Meet (Liberty, 1934)
World Gone Mad (Majestic, 1933)
You Can't Beat Love (RKO, 1937)

Albert Herman
(Adam H. Foelker) (1887–1967)

Arizona Frontier (Monogram, 1940)
Bad Men of Thunder Gap (PRC, 1943)
Bars of Hate (Victory, 1936)
Big Boy Rides Again (Beacon/First Division, 1935)
The Big Chance (Eagle, 1933)
Blazing Justice (Spectrum, 1936)
The Clutching Hand (Stage & Screen, 1936) (Serial)
Cowboy and the Bandit (International/Superior, 1935)
Danger Ahead (Victory, 1935)
Delinquent Daughters (PRC, 1944)
Down the Wyoming Trail (Monogram, 1939)
Exposed (Independent, 1932)
Gentleman from Dixie (Monogram, 1941)
The Golden Trail (Monogram, 1940)

Gun Play (Lucky Boots) (Beacon/First Division, 1935)
Hot Off the Press (Victory, 1935)
Man from Texas (Monogram, 1939)
Miss V. from Moscow (PRC, 1942)
The Missing Corpse (PRC, 1945)
Nazi Spy Ring (Dawn Express) (PRC, 1942)
Outlaws of the Range (Spectrum, 1936)
Pals of the Silver Sage (Monogram, 1940)
The Phantom of 42nd Street (PRC, 1945. Also associate producer)
The Pioneers (Monogram, 1941)
Rainbow over the Range (Monogram, 1940)
The Rangers Take Over (PRC, 1943)
Renfrew of the Great White Trail (Grand National, 1938)
Renfrew of the Royal Mounted (Grand National, 1937. Also producer)
Rhythm of the Rio Grande (Monogram, 1940)
Rogue's Gallery (PRC, 1945. Also co-producer)
Roll Wagons Roll (Monogram, 1939)
Rollin' Home to Texas (Monogram, 1941)
Rollin' Plains (Grand National, 1938)
Rollin' Westward (Monogram, 1939)
Shake Hands with Murder (PRC, 1944)
Song of the Buckaroo (Monogram, 1939)
Sporting Chance (Independent, 1931)
Starlight Over Texas (Monogram, 1938)
Sundown on the Prairie (Monogram, 1939)
Take Me Back to Oklahoma (Monogram, 1940)
Trail's End (Beaumont, 1935)
Twisted Rails (Imperial, 1935)
Utah Trail (Grand National, 1938)
Valley of Terror (Ambassador-Conn., 1937)
Western Frontier (Columbia, 1935)
What Price Crime? (Beacon, 1935)
Where the Buffalo Roam (Monogram, 1938)

A duel is arranged in this scene from Albert Herman's "Phantom of 42nd Street" (Alan Mowbray on right).

The Whispering Shadow (Mascot, 1933. With Colbert Clark) (Serial)
A Yank in Libya (PRC, 1942)

Sam Newfield
(Samuel Neufeld) — also directed as Sherman Scott and Peter Stewart) (1899–1964)

Aces and Eights (Puritan, 1936)
Adventure Island (Paramount, 1947. As Peter Stewart)
Along the Mohawk Trail (ITC, 1956)
Along the Sundown Trail (PRC, 1942. As Peter Stewart)
Apology for Murder (PRC, 1945)
Arizona Gang Busters (PRC, 1940. As Peter Stewart)
Arizona Gunfighter (Republic, 1937)
Bar Z Bad Man (Republic, 1937)
Beasts of Berlin (Goose Step, Hell's Devils) (PDC, 1939. As Sherman Scott)
Beggar's Holiday (Tower, 1934)
Big Time or Bust (Tower, 1934)
Billy the Kid in "Cattle Stampede" (PRC, 1943)
Billy the Kid in "Fugitive of the Plains" (PRC, 1943)
Billy the Kid in "Law and Order" (PRC, 1943. As Sherman Scott)
Billy the Kid in Santa Fe (PRC, 1941. As Sherman Scott)
Billy the Kid in Texas (PRC, 1940. As Peter Stewart)
Billy the Kid in "The Kid Rides Again" (PRC, 1943. As Sherman Scott)
Billy the Kid in "The Mysterious Rider" (PRC, 1943. As Sherman Scott)
Billy the Kid in "The Renegade" (PRC, 1943)
Billy the Kid in "Western Cyclone" (PRC, 1943)

Billy the Kid Outlawed (PRC, 1940. As Peter Stewart)

Billy the Kid Trapped (PRC, 1942. As) Sherman Scott)

Billy the Kid Wanted (PRC, 1941. As Sherman Scott)

Billy the Kid's Fighting Pals (PRC, 1941. As Sherman Scott)

Billy the Kid's Gun Justice (PRC, 1940. As Peter Stewart)

Billy the Kid's Range War (PRC, 1941. As Peter Stewart)

Billy the Kid's Roundup (PRC, 1941. As Sherman Scott)

Billy the Kid's Smoking Guns (PRC, 1942. As Sherman Scott)

The Black Raven (PRC, 1943)

Blazing Frontier (PRC, 1943)

Blonde for a Day (PRC, 1946)

Boothill Brigade (Republic, 1937)

Border Badmen (PRC, 1945)

Border Caballero (Puritan, 1936)

Border Roundup (PRC, 1943)

Bulldog Courage (Puritan, 1935)

Burning Gold (Republic, 1936)

Code of the Cactus (Victory, 1939)

Code of the Mounted (Ambassador, 1935)

Code of the Plains (Eagle-Lion, 1947)

Code of the Rangers (Monogram, 1938)

The Colorado Kid (Republic, 1937)

The Contender (PRC, 1944)

The Counterfeiters (20th–Fox, 1948. As Peter Stewart)

Danger! Women at Work (PRC, 1943)

Dead Men Walk (PRC, 1943)

Desert Patrol (Republic, 1938)

The Devil Riders (PRC, 1943)

The Devil's Weed (Wild Weed) (Jewell, 1949. As Sherman Scott)

Doomed at Sundown (Republic, 1937)

The Drifter (PRC, 1942)

Durango Valley Raiders (Republic, 1938)

Federal Agent (Republic, 1936)

The Feud Maker (Republic, 1938)

Fighting Bill Carson (PRC, 1945)

Fighting Mad (Monogram, 1939)

The Fighting Renegade (Victory, 1939)

Fingerprints Don't Lie (Lippert, 1951)

Flaming Frontier (20th–Fox, 1958; Canada. Also producer)

Flaming Lead (Colony, 1939)

The Flying Serpent (PRC, 1946. As Sherman Scott)

Frontier Crusader (PRC, 1940. As Peter Stewart)

Frontier Fighters (Eagle-Lion, 1947)

Frontier Gambler (Associated, 1956)

Frontier Outlaws (PRC, 1944)

Frontier Scout (Grand National, 1938)

Fuzzy Settles Down (PRC, 1944)

The Gambler and the Lady (Lippert, 1952. With Patrick Jenkins; England)

The Gambling Terror (Republic, 1937)

Gangster's Den (PRC, 1945)

Gashouse Kids (PRC, 1946)

Ghost of Hidden City (PRC, 1946)

Ghost of Hidden Valley (PRC, 1947)

Ghost Patrol (Puritan, 1936)

Go-Get-'Em Haines (Puritan, 1936)

Gun Code (PRC, 1940. As Peter Stewart)

Gun Lords of Stirrup Basin (Republic, 1937)

Guns in the Dark (Republic, 1937)

Harlem on the Prairie (Associated Features, 1938)

Harvest Melody (PRC, 1943)

Hi-Jacked (Lippert, 1950)

His Brother's Ghost (PRC, 1945)

Hold That Woman! (PRC, 1940. As Sherman Scott)

I Accuse My Parents (PRC, 1944)

I Take This Oath (PRC, 1940. As Sherman Scott)

Important Witness (Tower, 1933)

The Invisible Killer (PDC, 1939. As Sherman Scott)

Jungle Siren (PRC, 1942)

The Kid Sister (PRC, 1945)

Lady at Midnight (Eagle-Lion, 1948. As Sherman Scott)

Mary Beth Hughes and Robert Lowell get a stern talking-to from the bench in "I Accuse My Parents."

Lady Chaser (PRC, 1946)

The Lady Confesses (PRC, 1945)

Lady in the Fog (Scotland Yard Inspector) (Lippert, 1952; England)

Larceny in Her Heart (PRC, 1946)

Last of the Desperados (Associated, 1956)

A Lawman Is Born (Republic, 1937)

Leave It to the Marines (Lippert, 1951)

Lightnin' Bill Carson (Puritan, 1936)

Lightning Carson Rides Again (Victory, 1938)

Lightning Raiders (PRC, 1945)

The Lions Den (Puritan, 1936)

The Lone Rider Ambushed (PRC, 1941)

The Lone Rider and the Bandit (PRC, 1941)

The Lone Rider Crosses the Rio (PRC, 1941)

The Lone Rider Fights Back (PRC, 1941)

The Lone Rider in Cheyenne (PRC, 1942)

The Lone Rider in "Death Rides the Plains" (PRC, 1943)

The Lone Rider in Frontier Fury (PRC, 1941)

The Lone Rider in "Ghost Town" (PRC, 1941)

The Lone Rider in "Law of the Saddle" (PRC, 1943)

The Lone Rider in "Overland Stagecoach" (PRC, 1943)

The Lone Rider in "Raiders of Red Gap" (PRC, 1943)

The Lone Rider in Texas Justice (PRC, 1942)

The Lone Rider in "Wild Horse Rustlers" (PRC, 1943)

The Lone Rider in "Wolves of the

Range" (PRC, 1943)

The Lone Rider Rides On (PRC, 1941)

The Long Rifle and the Tomahawk (ITC, 1956. With Sidney Salkow)

The Lost Continent (Lippert, 1951)

The Mad Monster (PRC, 1942)

Marked Men (PRC, 1940. As Sherman Scott)

Marrying Widows (Tower, 1934)

Mask of the Dragon (Lippert, 1951)

Melody of the Plains (Spectrum, 1937)

Money Madness (Film Classics, 1948. As Peter Stewart)

The Monster Maker (PRC, 1944)

Motor Patrol (Lippert, 1950)

Murder Is My Business (PRC, 1946)

Nabonga (PRC, 1944)

Northern Frontier (Ambassador, 1935)

Oath of Vengeance (PRC, 1944)

Outlaw of the Plains (PRC, 1945)

Outlaw Women (Lippert, 1952. With Ron Ormond)

Outlaws of Boulder Pass (PRC, 1943)

Outlaws of the Rio Grande (PRC, 1941. As Peter Stewart)

Outlaws Paradise (Victory, 1939)

Overland Riders (PRC, 1946)

Paroled-to-Die (Republic, 1938)

The Pathfinder and the Mohican (ITC, 1956)

The Phantom Ranger (Monogram, 1938)

Prairie Badmen (PRC, 1946)

Prairie Pals (PRC, 1943. As Peter Stewart)

Prairie Rustlers (PRC, 1945)

Queen of Broadway (PRC, 1943)

Queen of Burlesque (PRC, 1946)

Racing Luck (Republic, 1935)

Radar Secret Service (Lippert, 1950)

Raiders of Red Rock (Eagle-Lion, 1947)

Raiders of the West (PRC, 1942. As Peter Stewart)

Rangers Roundup (Spectrum, 1938)

The Redman and the Renegades (ITC, 1956)

Reform Girl (Tower, 1933)

Riders of Black Mountain (PRC, 1940. As Peter Stewart)

Ridin' the Lone Trail (Republic, 1937)

Roarin' Guns (Puritan, 1936)

Roarin' Lead (Republic, 1936. With Mack V. Wright)

Rolling Down the Great Divide (PRC, 1942. As Peter Stewart)

Rustler's Hideout (PRC, 1944)

The Sagebrush Family Trail West (PDC, 1939. As Peter Stewart)

Secrets of a Model (Continental, 1940)

Sheriff of Sage Valley (PRC, 1943. As Sherman Scott)

Six Gun Rhythm (Grand National, 1938)

Six Gun Trail (Victory, 1938)

Skipalong Rosenbloom (Eagle-Lion, 1951)

Sky High (Lippert, 1951)

Songs and Bullets (Republic, 1938)

Stagecoach Outlaws (PRC, 1945)

State Department File 649 (Film Classics, 1949. As Peter Stewart)

Stormy Trails (Grand National, 1936)

Straight Shooter (Victory, 1940)

The Strange Mrs. Crane (Eagle-Lion, 1948. As Sherman Scott)

Swing Hostess (PRC, 1944)

Terror of Tiny Town (Astor, 1938)

Terrors on Horseback (PRC, 1946)

Texas Manhunt (PRC, 1942. As Peter Stewart)

The Texas Marshal (PRC, 1941. As Peter Stewart)

Texas Renegades (PRC, 1940. As Peter Stewart)

Texas Wildcats (Victory, 1939)

Three Desperate Men (Lippert, 1951)

The Three Outlaws (Associated, 1956)

Three on a Ticket (PRC, 1947)

Thunder in the Desert (Republic, 1938)

Thunder Over Sangoland (Lippert, 1954)

Thundering Gun Slingers (PRC, 1944)

Tiger Fangs (PRC, 1943)

Timber War (Ambassador, 1935)

Trail of Vengeance (Republic, 1937)

Trails of the Wild (Caryl of the Mountains) (Ambassador, 1935)

The Traitor (Puritan, 1936)

Trigger Fingers (Victory, 1939)

Trigger Pals (Grand National, 1939)

Top: Arline Judge argues her case for prison reform in "Girls in Chains." Bottom: Margaret Lindsay (left) and Nancy Coleman in "Her Sister's Secret." Both films directed by Edgar G. Ulmer.

Tumbleweed Trail (PRC, 1942)

Under Secret Orders (Progressive, 1933)

Valley of Vengeance (PRC, 1944)

Western Pacific Agent (Lippert, 1950)

White Pongo (PRC, 1945)

The Wild Dakotas (Associated, 1956. With Sigmund Neufeld; also co-producer)

Wild Horse Phantom (PRC, 1944)

Wolf Dog (20th–Fox, 1958; Canada. Also producer)

Edgar George Ulmer
(1904–1972)

The Amazing Transparent Man (AIP, 1961)

Americaner Schaden (The Marriage Broker) (Collective, 1939. In Yiddish)

Babes in Bagdad (United Artists, 1952)

The Black Cat (The Vanishing Body) Universal, 1934. Also co-story, set designer)

Bluebeard (PRC, 1944)

Carnegie Hall (United Artists, 1947)

Club Havana (PRC, 1945)

Damaged Lives (Weldon, 1933. Also co-story)

Daughter of Dr. Jekyll (Allied Artists, 1957)

Detour (PRC, 1945)

Die Klatsche (The Light Ahead) (Collective, 1939. In Yiddish)

Fishke der Drume (Germany, 1939)

From 9 to 9 (Independent, 1935)

Girls in Chains (PRC, 1943. Also story)

Greene Felde (Green Fields) Collective, 1937. With Jacob Ben-Ami. Also producer. In Yiddish)

Hannibal (Warner Bros., 1960. With Carlo Ludovico Bragaglia; also producer; Italy)

Helden Himmel und Holle (Settle Contro la Morte; The Cavern) (20th–Fox, 1964. Germany/Italy. With Paolo Bianchini; also producer)

Her Sister's Secret (PRC, 1946)

Isle of Forgotten Sins (Monsoon) (PRC, 1943. Also story)

Jive Junction (PRC, 1943)

L'Atlantide (Journey Beneath the Desert) (Italy, 1961. Italian title: *Antinea/l'amante della citta sepolta.* Released in England in 1964 under the title *The Lost Kingdom.* Released in the United States in 1965 by Embassy under the title *Journey Beneath the Desert.* With Guiseppe Masini, and uncredited Frank Borzage)

The Man from Planet X (United Artists, 1951)

Menschen am Sonntag (People on Sunday) (Film Studio, 1929. Germany. With Robert Siodmak)

Mister Broadway (Broadway-Hollywood, 1933)

Moon Over Harlem (Meteor, 1939)

Murder Is My Beat (Dynamite Anchorage) (Allied Artists, 1955)

My Son, the Hero (PRC, 1943. Also co-script)

The Naked Dawn (Universal, 1954)

Natalka Poltavka (Collective, 1937. In Yiddish)

The Perjurer (Gloria Films, 1957. Germany)

The Pirates of Capri (Captain Sirocco) (Film Classics, 1949. Italy)

Ruthless (Eagle-Lion, 1948)

St. Benny the Dip (United Artists, 1951)

Strange Illusion (Out of the Night) (PRC, 1945)

The Strange Woman (United Artists, 1946)

Thunder Over Texas (Beacon, 1934. As John Warner)

The Time Barrier (AIP, 1960)

Tomorrow We Live (PRC, 1942)

The Wife of Monte Crisco (PRC, 1946. Also co-adaptation)

Yenkel dem Schmidt (The Singing Blacksmith) (Collective, 1938. In Yiddish)

Zaporosh Sa Dunayem (Cossacks Across the Danube) (Avramenko Films, 1938)

Jean Yarbrough
(1900–1975)

According to Mrs. Hoyle (Monogram, 1951)
Angels in Disguise (Monogram, 1949)
Big Timber (Monogram, 1950)
The Brute Man (PRC, 1946)
Casa Manana (Monogram, 1951)
Caught in the Act (PRC, 1941)
The Challenge (20th–Fox, 1948)
City Limits (Monogram, 1941)
Crashing Las Vegas (Allied Artists, 1956)
The Creeper (20th–Fox, 1948)
Criminal Investigator (Monogram, 1942)
Cuban Pete (Universal, 1946)
The Devil Bat (PRC, 1940)
Father Makes Good (Monogram, 1951)
Father Steps Out (Monogram, 1941)
Follow the Band (Universal, 1943)
Footsteps in the Night Allied Artists, 1957)
Freckles Comes Home (Monogram, 1942)
The Gang's All Here (Monogram, 1941)
Get Going (Universal, 1943)
Good Morning, Judge (Universal, 1943)
Henry, the Rainmaker (Monogram, 1949)
Here Come the Co-eds (Universal, 1945)
Hi Ya, Sailor (Universal, 1943. Also producer)
Hillbillys in a Haunted House (Woolner Bros., 1967)
Holiday in Havana (Monogram, 1949)
Hot Shots (Allied Artists, 1956)
House of Horrors (Universal, 1946)
In Society (Universal, 1944)
Inside Job (Universal, 1946. Also producer)
Jack and the Beanstalk (Universal, 1952)
Joe Palooka in "Humphrey Takes a Chance" (Monogram, 1950)

Joe Palooka Meets Humphrey (Monogram, 1950)
King of the Zombies (Monogram, 1941)
Law of the Jungle (Monogram, 1942)
Leave It to Henry (Monogram, 1949)
Let's Go Collegiate (Monogram, 1941)
Lost in Alaska (Universal, 1952)
Lure of the Islands (Monogram, 1942)
Man from Headquarters (Monogram, 1942)
Master Minds (Monogram, 1949)
Moon Over Las Vegas (Universal, 1944. Also producer)
The Mutineers (Monogram, 1949)
The Naughty Nineties (Universal, 1945)
Night Freight (Allied Artists, 1954)
On Stage, Everybody (Universal, 1945)
Police Bullets (Monogram, 1942)
Rebellious Daughters (Progressive, 1938)
Saintly Sinners (United Artists, 1962)
Shed No Tears (Eagle-Lion, 1948)
She's in the Army (Monogram, 1942)
She-Wolf of London (Universal, 1946)
Sideshow (Monogram, 1950)
Silent Witness (Monogram, 1942)
So's Your Aunt Emma (Meet the Mob) (Monogram, 1942)
So's Your Uncle (Universal, 1943. Also producer)
South of Dixie (Universal, 1944)
South of Panama (PRC, 1941)
Square Dance Katy (Monogram, 1950)
Top Sergeant Mulligan (Monogram, 1941)
Triple Threat (Columbia, 1948)
Triple Trouble (Monogram, 1950)
Twilight on the Prairie (Universal, 1944)
Under Western Skies (Universal, 1945)
Week-end Pass (Universal, 1944)
The Women of Pitcairn Island (20th–Fox, 1956)
Yaqui Drums (Allied Artists, 1956)

An Interview with Edgar G. Ulmer

Conducted by Peter Bogdanovich

EGU: (Leon) Fromkess had come out and the whole PRC thing was collapsing. I met Fromkess, who was an accountant then, through my connection with Pathé Lab. Pathé put me in charge of the whole program with Seymour [Nebenzal] helping me. The first script they gave me was *Prisoner of Japan*, which already had a contract for a director named [Arthur] Ripley. So I had to produce the picture, rewrite the script, and finally shoot the picture the last two days of the six days he shot. Through that I drifted into PRC and couldn't get out. I did so many pictures for them. What helped me at PRC was that number 1: I could use my crew, and I nearly was running the studio from a technical end. The little *Girls in Chains* [1943] was such a gigantic money success that we could have bought the PRC Studio. I wouldn't sign any contract with PRC, but this was my home and I could operate and bring any idea immediately to the top echelon. I suffered, of course, from one thing. I was so tied up that I couldn't take any contracts on the outside. . . . At that time I was called "the Capra of PRC." It was a nice family feeling, not too much interference — if there was interference, it was only that we had no money, that was all. . . . Most of my PRC pictures were made in six days. Just try to visualize it — eighty setups a day.

PB: Really? I once did forty and almost died. How can you do eighty?

EGU: Ask my wife — she's my script supervisor. I was known all over town. I could have gone anywhere, but I was under exclusive contract. There would come a time around four o'clock in the afternoon when I would say, "Aces wild, we go into a PRC hour now, I'll give the numbers." But I had a perfect technique worked out. No set of mine existed in these pictures where one wall was not without any paintings, without anything, just a plain wall in gray. I shot my master scene, but left for the last day the close-ups. They would play against that one flat, blank wall, and I would say "camera left," "camera right." They would say two sentences, I would hold my hand in front of the lens not to stop the camera, and he would go into the second speech, because I couldn't afford to go through. I had to cut with the camera, because I was only

63

Top: Sally Eilers (left) comforts a bewildered Mary McLeod in Edgar Ulmer's "Out of the Night" ("Strange Illusion"). Bottom: Regis Toomey (left), Jimmy Lydon, and John Hamilton (later to appear in the "Superman" TV series) in "Out of the Night."

allowed 15,000 feet for a feature. No more. Two to one, nothing more.

PB: So you didn't even bother to slate. You put your hand in.

EGU: Yes. I laughed when I came over to Italy to make my first picture and they bragged about their fast slates. Because in the beginning, when they didn't have the raw stock, they wouldn't spend more than two feet. I laughed. I said, "You think that's fast?" I showed them how to do it.

. . . Fromkess became head of the studio; he would listen, and when I would say I want to make a *Bluebeard* (1944), that's what we would make.

PB: *Hitler's Madman* was directed by Douglas Sirk, wasn't it?

EGU: It was his first [American] picture — I hired him for that. It was sold to MGM after it was made.

PB: It was a very good picture but you received no credit, did you?

EGU: None.

PB: But you worked on the script?

EGU: Script and sets.

PB: . . . Evidently you worked on the scripts of some pictures at PRC which you didn't direct — like *Corregidor*.

EGU: Correct. *Corregidor, Danger! Women at Work* [both 1943] — there was a whole slew of these things.

PB: For which you sometimes didn't take credit?

EGU: No, I couldn't.

PB: *Girls in Chains* I saw, and you said it was made in five days?

EGU: Yah.

PB: Incredible. Do you remember how the idea for that came about?

EGU: This came from the newspaper. There was some political graft in one of the women's jails. There was a lot of newspaper coverage on it, and I thought up the title. Fromkess and his right-hand man, Martin Mooney, felt that we had a big chance with the thing. The script was written in something like three weeks.

PB: The title is very commercial.

EGU: Of course! That's what made the goddamned thing. At the beginning of the season, Fromkess would sit down with me and [Sig] Neufeld, and we would invent forty-eight titles. We didn't have stories yet; they had to be written to fit the cockeyed titles. I am convinced when I look back that all this was a challenge. I knew that nothing was impossible. When *Double Indemnity* [1944] came out and was a huge success, I wrote a picture for Neufeld that we called *Single Indemnity*. We were able to write that junk in about two weeks.

PB: The picture was not made?

EGU: Oh, yes, it was made, but not with that title. Paramount made us take the title off! I think it was called *Blond Ice*, or something like that.

PB: You didn't direct it?

EGU: No.

Arline Judge (standing, second from left) is appalled when Anne Seymour (guard at center) demonstrates discipline in the women's prison in Edgar Ulmer's "Girls in Chains."

PB: *Isle of Forgotten Sins* [1943], what was what?

EGU: That was a hangover I had left from the time I was with Murnau in Bora Bora on *Tabu* [1931].

PB: *Tabu* — did you work on that?

EGU: Yes, of course. And then John Ford made the picture for Sam Goldwyn called *The Hurricane* [1937]. The miniature department had about two hundred palm trees; I knew I could persuade them to borrow the miniatures for a picture — so I wrote *Isle of Forgotten Sins*.

PB: So that you could use the miniatures?!

EGU: Correct.

PB: You were having fun over there, it seems, at PRC. What did you do on *Tabu*?

EGU: I worked on the script with Murnau, got all his equipment down there, and set up the production for him. When he came back, I cut the picture and got it ready for Eisenfeld to score it.

PB: And [Robert] Flaherty did very little on the picture?

EGU: Flaherty was sent back after the first four weeks. They couldn't get along. The drunk Irishman on one side and the German educated at Oxford on the other. Murnau was a very, very difficult man, but a great, great talent.

PB: And then what about *Jive Junction* [1943]? I saw *Jive Junction* — I don't think that's one of your best pictures.

EGU: No. You saw the conflict I brought into that script. I wanted classical music against jive, and you couldn't do it for the little money I had. And, of course, it was propaganda to get the kids in America working on the farms during the war.

PB: I see in the credits that Irving Wallace had something to do with the story — was that the Irving Wallace who became a novelist?

EGU: Yes, sir.

PB: How did you feel, making pictures like these — so quickly and with a subject matter not always of the most distinction?

EGU: I had to compromise to keep PRC in business. Now I admit to myself that I was somehow schizophrenic in making pictures. On one hand, I was absolutely concerned with box office and on the other, I was trying to create art and decency, with a style. I could not completely get out of the commercial though I knew it limited me. There was no reason for me to make a *Jive Junction*, except that the picture had to be made, and had to be done quickly, and we couldn't jeopardize a penny.

PB: Yes. Then I suppose that even things like *Girls in Chains* and *Isle of Forgotten Sins* fall into that commercial category, whereas *Bluebeard* falls into the other.

EGU: Yes. You can tell by the cameraman I had on the picture if I took a picture very seriously or not. For my serious pictures I always had [Eugen] Schüfftan.

PB: Was he on *Bluebeard*?

EGU: Yes.

PB: Who is Jockey Feindel?

EGU: Feindel was actually the operative cameraman, because Schüfftan never could get into the union.

PB: So he couldn't take credit.

EGU: Of course not. He took the Academy Award as you know for the best photography, on Paul Newman's picture with Jackie Gleason . . . *The Hustler* [1960]. Schüfftan still isn't in the union.

PB: Hm. And so he shot *Bluebeard*.

EGU: Yah.

PB: Did he shoot *Detour*?

EGU: No, *Detour* was shot by my old friend Benny Kline. He shot *The Wife of Monte Cristo* for me and *Strange Illusion* [1945].

PB: Now, how did you get the idea for *Bluebeard*? That's one of your best pictures, I think.

EGU: Yes. It was a tremendously challenging picture.

PB: Shot quickly?

EGU: Very quickly — six days.

PB: Amazing. It had a remarkable sense of mood and atmosphere.

Poster for Edgar Ulmer's "The Wife of Monte Cristo."

EGU: Yah. All my love for Paris came out in the picture.

PB: And you created Paris on the back lot?

EGU: Of course. I did the sets myself as I did in *The Wife of Monte Cristo*. As an art director, from my earliest time on, I adored the Ile-de-France, Montparnasse and Montmartre, and whatever I did I always wound up in that. I adore Paris. I spent two years of my youth in the Victorine in Nice. I was there with Rex Ingram.

PB: Yes, you told me. Well, *Bluebeard* has an incredible style. I really think it's one of your best pictures.

EGU: Yah. First of all, John Carradine was a person, like Arthur Kennedy, I could hang onto. He knew what we were trying to do. Yah, it was a very lovely picture. PRC was unhappy with it at first.

PB: Really. But it did finally make some money.

EGU: Of course. It was one of the pictures that earned tremendous money in France.

PB: The title is a very commercial title actually.

EGU: Yah. I had a fight with Chaplin about that title—I beat Chaplin out of it. He was making *Monsieur Verdoux* [1947]. I think my picture was nicer. *Monsieur Verdoux* was a horrible picture.

PB: After *Bluebeard*, you made *Strange Illusion*. How did the idea for that come about?

EGU: [Fritz] Rotter's play in New York, *Letters from Lucerne*, with Gerte Mosheim, was a big flop. I saw it and it was very nice, though not well written—Rotter mostly did musical comedies. I got Fromkess to buy the play; but when we wrote the script I went so far away from Rotter's play that we sold it back to him! I was fascinated at that time with psychoanalysis and this story was about a father-son relationship. The picture was very well received critically. Whether it made money, I do not know. At that time I was already chafing at the bit and wanted *out* of PRC.

PB: But you stayed there for another five or six pictures?

EGU: Oh, yah. Fromkess really locked me in.

PB: There are some very interesting shots in there; I remember one in particular—there's a painting on the wall and you pan around it. Do you remember that shot?

EGU: Yah.

PB: Was it made very quickly also?

EGU: Six days.

PB: Incredible. Now, *Club Havana* [1946] . . .

EGU: . . . That I adored making. I loved it. I had no script—I did a Rossellini again. This was a picture I was never going to make; Russell Rouse and Clarence Greene were going to make it. Fromkess had hired a whole staff and everything, and then threw the script out a week before we were to shoot. He called me in and said, "OK, you say you can do things. Shoot it without a script—invent it." So I got myself some actors. I had only one page — an outline. Schüfftan did that picture for me, too.

I really had fun on that one; we shot the whole picture on one set. We had quite a musical success with the cockeyed thing. "Tico Tico" was used in that the first time.

PB: So the challenge was not the subject matter, but just to make something?

EGU: No! To make something special — to be able to do a *Grand Hotel* [1932] in one place.

PB: This was PRC's *Grand Hotel — Club Havana.*

EGU: Yah.

PB: Very funny. Where did the idea come for *Detour*, which is my favorite of your films?

EGU: Now, I'm going to tell you something strange. The brother-in-law of Tony Quinn wrote a very bad book called *Detour*. [Martin] Goldsmith was his name. I took the thing to Martin Mooney and rewrote the script. I was always in love with the idea and with the main character, a boy who plays piano in Greenwich Village and really wants to be a decent pianist. He's so down on his luck that the girl who goes to the Coast is the only person he can exist with sex-wise — the "Blue Angel" thing. And then the idea to get involved on that long road into Fate, where he's an absolute loser, fascinated me. The same thing, of course, with the boy who played the leading character, Tom Neal. He wound up in jail after he killed his own wife. He did practically the same thing he did in the picture.

PB: Surely not with a telephone cord.

EGU: No, that was the only thing he didn't do.

PB: That was one of the most memorable murders because it's a murder by long distance, through the door, and so on. Was that one of your ideas?

EGU: Yah.

PB: A very grisly touch. Ann Savage was an excellent character. How fast did you shoot that?

EGU: Six days.

PB: All these pictures were made in six days — one week?

EGU: Sure. The only one that took two weeks was *The Wife of Monte Cristo —*

PB: Because it was a costume picture?

EGU: Because it was a *big* picture.

PB: Big picture — two weeks! Are you fond of *Detour*, yourself?

EGU: I adore *Detour.*

PB: Which are your favorite pictures?

EGU: *Black Cat, Detour,* and *Naked Dawn.*

PB: *Naked Dawn* is a remarkable film.

EGU: Also shot in ten days.

Ulmer's "Club Havana" was intended to be PRC's answer to MGM's "Grand Hotel."

PB: In color?

EGU: Yes, sir.

PB: Incredible. That was released by U-I but not made for U-I?

EGU: Right.

PB: Now what about *The Wife of Monte Cristo* — how did that come about?

EGU: Fromkess called me in one day and told me that Eddie Small was making a fortune with *The Son of Monte Cristo* [1940], in fact, with all the family of Monte Cristo. He said he wanted to make a Monte Cristo also, so we decided to make the "Wife."

PB: I see — so it had very little to do with Dumas.

EGU: Actually there is a very bad novel by Dumas, placed in Arabia, called *The Wife of Monte Cristo*.

PB: I've never seen it; how is it?

EGU: It's a nice picture. It's better than the one Eddie Small made.

PB: And was that shot by Schüfftan, too?

EGU: Yah.

PB: And who was Adolph Kull, who got the credit?

EGU: He was one of the operators.

PB: Terrible that Schüfftan couldn't get credit. It's awful.

EGU: It's a pity. He has credit on every European print.

PB: Ah, I see. What is *Her Sister's Secret* [1946]? That was really quite a good picture.

EGU: Yes. That was a remake of a German picture. It was the first American job of the cameraman Franz Planer, a Viennese, who had worked with me in 1920.

PB: On what?

EGU: *Sodom and Gomorrah.*

PB: Was that a movie?

EGU: Yes. Directed by Michael Curtiz, at that time he was Mishka Kehrtez. It was done in Vienna, sets by Julius Borsidine and myself.

PB: *The Strange Woman* [1946] is a difficult film to get to see, but Schüfftan gets credit as producer on it.

EGU: Schüfftan was not on *The Strange Woman* at all. Beautiful picture. It nearly got Hedy Lamarr an Academy nomination. It's the only picture where she ever had to act. A beautiful picture. Very difficult, very beautiful.

PB: That was the first picture away from PRC?

EGU: Yah. *Her Sister's Secret* was the last picture for PRC.

PB: Did you leave them amicably?

EGU: Yes. I was under contract to them. They got the money for *The Strange Woman* — not me. I got $250 a week, and they were collecting $1,500. I made more money for PRC on *The Strange Woman* than they had paid me the whole time I worked there.

"B" Movie Structure

by Charles Flynn and Todd McCarthy

Some five thousand full-length theatrical motion pictures were produced and released in the United States between 1930 and 1939 and an additional four thousand were made between 1940 and 1949.

The sheer volume of Hollywood's output in these two decades is paralleled in few other art forms. And, like the flourishing of painting in fifteenth-century Florence or the glory of the novel in Victorian England, the Golden Age of the movies was the product of some very definite economic circumstances.

For one thing, the Golden Age was, qualitatively, far from "golden." A very small proportion of the films produced in the 1930s and the 1940s is remembered today. We still see the star vehicles and the personal works of the great directors (Ford, Hawks, Walsh, Cukor, McCarey, et al.), but the overwhelming proportion of Hollywood films of the 1930s and 1940s were strictly workhorses: films designed to pay the rent and light bills.

This, indeed, implies a financial analysis that may be beyond the scope of this essay or even of this book. The definitive financial history of Hollywood has yet to be written, and this essay is hardly even a beginning. For one thing, our emphasis is almost exclusively on the studios that made "B" movies.

The group of disparate "B" studios was collectively called "The B-Hive" and "Gower Gulch." They thrived between 1935 and 1950. Today, film historians remember them as Poverty Row. Most of their products have been long forgotten; few of them appear even on television or at university film societies. And certainly few admirers of Jean-Luc Godard's "Breathless" (1959) have more than the foggiest notion of what Monogram Pictures (to which the film is jokingly dedicated) was.

A few of Poverty Row's directors have been resurrected, most notably Edgar G. Ulmer. But its organizing principles remain obscure.

Most people think of "B" movies (Ulmer's *Detour* [1946], for example) simply as low-budget films with formulaic plots.

73

Getting a light from Charles D. Bronson in "Apology for Murder" is Hugh Beaumont, later to appear as Ward Cleaver in television's "Leave It to Beaver."

Others may knowledgeably observe that the "B" movie was the
movie on the lower half of the double bill.

These definitions are both correct — but perhaps incomplete.

The reason the "B"s were the way they were (and why they existed
at all) was the system of exhibition of films in the United States in the
1930s and 1940s.

The Double Bill

From 1935 to about 1950, the American moviegoing audience ex-
pected a double bill of two complete features every time it attended the
movies. Added to this would be cartoons, a newsreel, and several trailers
(previews of coming attractions, so named because they "trailed" the
main feature and were often physically spliced onto its last reel).

It was the Depression-era moviegoer who first insisted on a complete
three-hour-plus program for his or her money, and the practice is a
logical outgrowth of the Depression state of mind. That more than a few
moviegoers often failed to sit through the entire program is beside the
point.

Ian MacDonald (left) looks a little uncomfortable accepting help from Richard Deane and Mary Hall in this scene from "Swamp Woman."

By 1932, many American theaters had started to present double bills, and by the end of 1935, the practice had proved so popular that eighty-five percent of the theaters in this country were presenting double bills. Only the most elegant first-run theaters in the major cities stuck to single features.

There had certainly been low-budget features before the arrival of the double bill, but, as we shall see, it was the double bill that made the "B"s a necessity.

Distribution: A Digression

As the double-bill era dawned, the system of movie distribution was very different from today's (and very profitable for the studios, while it lasted).

Five of the major studios (RKO, MGM, Twentieth Century–Fox, Warner Bros., and Paramount) owned large chains of theaters. Thus they controlled the means of exhibition as well as production and distribution. These five *vertically integrated* studios (in business terminology) controlled their products every step of the way, from creation through marketing to end use.

In a historic antitrust decision in 1948 (written by Associate Justice William O. Douglas), the Supreme Court decided that this type of vertical integration violated the antitrust laws, and ordered the five companies in question to sell off their theaters.

It gradually became apparent that the studios had been making a great deal of money on their theaters and very little on production and distribution, but that is another story.

The separation of exhibition from production/distribution took time, nearly five years. In order, this is how the studios divested themselves of their theaters:

Dec. 31, 1949: Paramount splits into Paramount Pictures Corporation and United Paramount Theatres.

Dec. 31, 1950: Radio-Keith-Orpheum Corporation (RKO) splits into RKO Pictures Corporation and RKO Theaters Corporation.

Feb. 6, 1952: MGM sells its theaters to Loews, Inc.

Sept. 27, 1952: Twentieth Century–Fox sells its theaters to National Theaters, Inc.

Feb. 28, 1953: Warner Bros. theaters acquired by newly formed Stanley Warner Corporation; WB stock splits two-for-one.

Until the divestiture order, a large part of the movie industry enjoyed *guaranteed* distribution. RKO films were booked into RKO theaters, Paramount films were booked into Paramount theaters, and so on. Each studio knew how many theaters it controlled and could rely on.

The studios knew, too, that they had what amounted to a guaranteed audience. Movie attendance had reached seventy-five million weekly by the end of the 1930s, had continued to climb during the war, and had finally peaked at an astounding one hundred million weekly — two-thirds of the total American population — in 1946. Two years later, weekly attendance had slipped to eighty-five million and had begun the long slide to forty million in 1957, finally bottoming out at about twenty million in the late 1960s and early 1970s.

Due largely to an almost complete lack of alternate sources of entertainment (except for radio, an equally vital but formally different medium), there was an overwhelming demand for movies in the 1930s and 1940s.

The guaranteed audience meant guaranteed bookings, and vice versa.

Enter the *"B" Movie*

The enviable position of the studios in relation to their audience and the theaters, coupled with the double bill, put the studios in something of a dilemma. They were more than willing to supply the top-of-the-bill drawing cards, the class features with big names like Gable, Cagney, Bogart, Tracy, Harlow, Davis, Crawford; but by and large, the major studios had neither the inclination nor the resources to supply the second feature. This was especially true in the 1940s, when rising production costs led the majors to abandon program pictures altogether.

It was clear that the top (or "A") feature would garner the lion's share of the box-office take. Thanks to the guaranteed distribution, there was practically no risk in producing the second (or "B") feature, but there were only modest profits. So the major studios found little or no financial reason for producing the "B" feature.

The reason for this was a system the major studios had developed in which the "A" feature played with a percentage of the box office take going to the producer/distributor, and the exhibitor taking the rest. (In the case of the integrated companies, this was more or less a bookkeeping exercise since all the money eventually found its way into the same till, but the production and exhibition divisions of these companies were managed separately.) The split might be 60/40 − 60 percent to the distributor, 40 percent to the theater. For an extremely popular film, the split might go to 80/20 or even 90/10. (Exhibitors can be heard to howl loud and long when the studios extract 90/10 deals for blockbusters like *The Godfather* [1972] and *The Exorcist* [1973].)

It is obvious why the studios didn't double bill two first-class pictures together. Why blow your wad on one throw, when you can extract two admissions for two films?

In contrast to the "A" picture's percentage deal, the bottom-half picture played for a flat (fixed) rental. Since the rental wasn't based on attendance or popularity, the producer could predict with great accuracy how much he would take in on each "B" picture. But the potential of spectacular gains on a smash hit was missing. That is why the major studios largely eschewed producing such films. However, there was little downside risk. A studio could produce a "B" picture for, say, $75,000 or $80,000 and clear $10,000 or $15,000 profit.

And, seeing that someone could make such a fairly certain profit supplying nothing but cheaply produced hour-long genre films for the bottom of the double bill, Republic, Monogram, and many other studios stepped in to garner the miniscule profits that the majors shunned.

FEATURE PICTURE PRODUCTION IN UNITED STATES 1940–45

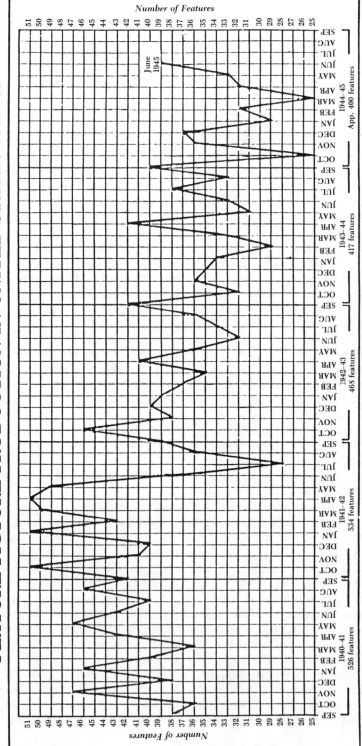

This graph charts the levels of feature picture production of American companies by months in each production period from that of 1940–41 and for the first six months of 1945; also given is the total number of features produced in each of these twelve-month periods and the indicated total for that of 1944–45. (Motion Picture Herald Chart)

A Digression: The States' Rights System

Many of the "B" studios, financially unable to set up a national system of company-owned distribution exchanges, farmed out the releasing of their product to independent distributors under the states' rights system.

Under this arrangement, a form of franchising, a studio sold the right to distribute its films on a territorial basis. Monogram in the 1930s, for example, might sell its films in the Southeast to a distributor in Atlanta, in the Midwest to a Chicago distributor, and so on.

The states' rights distributors were known as *franchisees*. A single firm, of course, could handle product from several studios, and most did.

Monogram and Republic studios eventually set up exchanges of their own in major cities, but almost all the other "B" studios used the states' rights system. It was the most economical method of distribution, because it required no outright advance investment by the producer for distribution (other than the cost of producing the film in the first place). Of course, the states' rights franchisees received a percentage of each film's income for their efforts.

In the 1930s, a leading states' rights outfit was First Division, which handled Monogram, Chesterfield, and Invincible studios. In the 1940s, Astor Pictures and Cavalcade Films were two of the most important independent distributors.

Even today, many independent producers, such as Russ Meyer and Roger Corman's New World Pictures, use the states' rights system. And there are still quite a few thriving states' rights distributors, such as Chicago's Jack Gilbreth and Atlanta's Jack Vaughan.

The "B" Studios

In addition to the five fully integrated majors, there were three other "semimajors." Columbia and Universal (Universal-International from 1946 to 1964) were producer/distributors; United Artists distributed only.

Then came the "B" studios. The two most important were Republic and Monogram. They both lasted from the mid-1930s into the 1950s. (And, indeed, they merged for a little over a year, from 1935 to 1936.) The products of these two studios epitomized the classical Hollywood "B" studio.

In addition to Monogram and Republic, small "B" studios proliferated just after the introduction of sound. There was a shake-out, with many studios going under, as the Depression bottomed out from 1932 to 1934. The situation gradually stabilized, and, by 1937, the three most important "B" studios were Republic, Monogram, and Grand National. The "B" phenomenon of the 1940s was Producers Releasing Corporation (PRC), but it was gone by 1947. The 1950s saw the end of Republic and Monogram and the formation of American-International Pictures. In the 1960s, a new wave of "B"-cum-exploitation outfits, including Cinemation, Fanfare, and Crown International, evolved.

One of the earliest of the second-rung studios was Tiffany, known as Tiffany-Stahl in the silent era (director John M. Stahl was also the studio's part owner and head of production . . . a very nice situation for a director!). Tiffany-Stahl's chief asset at that time was Mae Murray. Its product, mainly airy high-society pictures like Stahl's *Husbands and Lovers* (1924), would certainly have passed for "A" later on.

By 1931, however, Stahl had departed for Universal. Tiffany shifted its emphasis (due to the increased production costs necessitated by sound) to inexpensive Westerns, often with Phil Rosen or Al Rogell directing; but by the fall of 1932, Tiffany was in dire financial straits.

Sono Art–World Wide, another Poverty Row studio, bought Tiffany's remaining features as the Tiffany firm closed its doors. The same fate befell Sono Art–World Wide within a year. Twentieth Century–Fox bought out Sono Art–World Wide, which had been founded just three years before.

Many other obscure studios were casualties of the 1932 to 1934 era. Majestic, operated by an ambitious producer named Larry Darmour, folded in 1935, after three years in business. Its one notable release was Frank Strayer's *The Vampire Bat* (1933).

Chesterfield, founded in 1928, and Invincible, founded in 1932, shared office and studio space as well as financial connections. Both companies specialized in action and mystery melodramas; they folded in 1936.

Producer Ralph M. Like released his productions under the Action Pictures and Mayfair Pictures names; both firms disappeared in 1933. Similarly, producer M.H. Hoffman released under the Allied and Liberty names; he dropped both in 1934 to become a Monogram producer, and went, with Monogram, to Republic in 1935.

Victory Pictures (Sam Katzman's first enterprise), Puritan Pictures, Ambassador-Conn (Maurice Conn) — the pattern repeats itself over and over in the early 1930s. There were literally dozens of tiny studios, usually with impressive corporate names, that lasted two or three years and then disappeared.

The very high mortality rate among these infant studios is not surprising when we consider that a completely new industry (producing "B" pictures) was being born. It was a case of survival of the fittest, and one must admire the sheer determination of the many people who chose to start movie companies in the very depths of the Great Depression.

By 1934, it was clear that the two leading "B" studios were Mono-

June Clyde (left) witnesses a strange gathering in the breezy murder mystery "Seven Doors to Death."

gram, which had been founded by W. Ray Johnston in 1930, and Mascot, which Nat Levine had started in 1929. Mascot was a major source of serials and Monogram had a well-balanced "B" production program. By 1934, Monogram was producing thirty-six films a year.

It so happened that both firms were in debt to Consolidated Film Laboratories, a film-processing laboratory that handled many "B"s. CFL's owner, Herbert J. Yates, had decided that he wanted to run a movie studio. So he foreclosed on Monogram and Mascot and merged them into Republic Pictures (a name borrowed from a previous Yates lab) early in 1935.

Levine apparently was happy with this arrangement, and Mascot-style serials produced by Levine soon became a Republic staple. But after a couple of years, Johnston and his partner Trem Carr realized that they weren't getting along with the domineering Yates; so they left Republic and resurrected Monogram during 1936 and 1937. Johnston had been president of Republic, but was clearly subordinate to Yates, who was chairman of the board. In 1937, Levine became Republic's president, a position that he, like Johnston, held for less than two years.

By the end of 1937, the new Monogram had released twenty films. And a new "major minor" had appeared on the scene: Grand National. It was founded early in 1936 by Edward Alperson, a former film-exchange manager, who had managed to sign up James Cagney during one of the actor's periodic quarrels with Warners. Cagney appeared in John Blystone's *Great Guy* (1937), Grand National's one notable release. The firm did grind out quite a few forgettable pictures in its three-year history; it went bankrupt in 1939 after investing $900,000 in a Victor Schertzinger musical, *Something to Sing About*. Alperson shared Yates's and Johnston's ambitions; it was his financial mismanagement that sank Grand National.

Around the time of the Grand National collapse, another film-exchange manager, Ben Judell, decided to form a studio to produce "B"s and took over the former Grand National studios. After running through several names (Progressive Pictures, Producers Distributing Corporation, Sigmund Neufeld Productions) and a financial crisis (early in 1940, Judell's states' rights franchisees had to help the studio out of debt in order to obtain needed product), Judell finally arrived at a name he could live with: Producers Releasing Corporation.

PRC, which even owned some theaters, was the major competitor for Republic and Monogram throughout the 1940s. It produced several types of pictures: westerns, war films, mysteries, and musicals. It should be noted that both PRC and Monogram avoided the production of serials altogether.

By the end of the 1940s, demand for "B"s had dropped. PRC, always a marginal operation, was in trouble. In 1947, PRC was absorbed by Eagle-Lion, a distribution company owned by England's J. Arthur Rank. And so the PRC name disappeared. Four years later, United Artists bought out Eagle-Lion. Arthur Krim, Eagle-Lion president, became president of UA. Like Sono Art–World Wide, PRC was ultimately absorbed into a major . . . a rare occurrence.

Few of the producers and executives associated with "B" studios appear to have been men of great vision or artistic ambition. Most were doubtlessly motivated by a desire for profit. Their objective was to produce pure entertainment as cheaply as possible and to earn a tidy profit.

. . . Leon Fromkess is the name most often associated with PRC; he was its executive producer from 1942 to 1945 when director Edgar G. Ulmer was active at the studio.

Equally industrious in their day were the King brothers (né Maurice, Frank, and Herman Kozinski), who made an impressive string of hits, mostly topical crime thrillers, for PRC and Monogram, culminating in Monogram's *Dillinger* (1945). . . .

The men who financed and produced the "B"s had picked their niche, and they knew "B" production inside out.

Harry Davenport (center, with beard) supervises a rescue operation in one of the few color PRC films, "The Enchanted Forest."

Production and Finance

The "B" studios displayed endless imagination in their budget-cutting techniques. Inexpensive — and often inexpressive — acting, minimal sets, hack scripts, truncated shooting schedules all were standard.

Most "B" studio front offices reviewed scripts with a fine-tooth comb to eliminate bits of time-consuming business. A script called for the actor to light a cigarette in mid-scene? A fumble would call for a retake; the actor entered with the cigarette lit. In fact, as often as not, the scene would begin with our cigarette-puffing hero already in the room! (Why waste the time, and risk a retake, by having him open the door?)

This elimination of stage business, of entrances and exits, gives most "B"s a strange, almost cryptic air of flatness and unreality. The best of the "B" directors (Ulmer, Karlson, Dwan, Lewis, Ripley, Tourneur) developed a kind of visual shorthand to turn these minimal resources into expressive devices.

Edgar Ulmer's *Detour* (1946, PRC) has a cast of only two actors (Tom Neal and Ann Savage), one minimal hotel-room set (a bed and a window), and a back-projection screen displaying an endlessly moving highway scene.

Few "B" studios had any qualms about reusing footage from earlier productions, especially for such expensive-to-stage scenes as chases, fights, battles, and natural disasters. And many "B"s are liberally sprinkled with stock footage.

Indeed, perhaps the most audacious use ever of stock footage occurs in Ulmer's *Girls in Chains* (1943, PRC) — a classic women's prison picture, incidentally. A murder scene supposedly takes place late at night atop a dam. The actors involved play the scene in medium shot, with appropriately dim lighting, on a minimal set representing the catwalk atop the dam. The scene is *intercut* with stock footage of Hoover Dam, shot at high noon!

Republic serials were routinely rereleased under different titles. All in all, Republic made sixty-six serials in its twenty-two years, and most of them were seen more than once. The twelve-episode *The Phantom Rider* became *Ghost Riders of the West*; the fifteen-episode *Secret Service in Darkest Africa* became *Manhunt in the African Jungle*. (Spencer Gordon Bennet directed both, or all four, assisted by Fred Brannon on *The Phantom Rider*.) This trick was used more than once with features, too.

On another level, the director was under great pressure at a "B" studio. Budgets and schedules (important at every studio) were observed as Holy Writ. After all, a day or two over schedule, a thousand or two over budget could spell the difference between profit and loss for a "B." At an MGM, a speedy, slapdash director like W.S. ("One-Take Woody") Van Dyke was an oddity, a house joke. At a Monogram or a PRC, the second and third takes were extravagances.

In fact one PRC director, Sam Newfield (whose brother Sigmund Neufeld was PRC's executive producer), was so prolific that even PRC was embarrassed to have his name on so many of its releases. So Newfield used two aliases, "Peter Stewart" and "Sherman Scott" in rotation with his real name on his PRC films.

The best of the "B"s seem uniquely products of the "Zeitgeist" of the 1940s. The most memorable "B" images are of postwar urban America. Monogram's sparse expressionistic sets and PRC's generic, unchanging city-street set seem to sum up that brief time between World War II and the Korean War. . . .

However, the "B" movies and the "B" studios should always be remembered as the ultimate expression of that brief time when Hollywood was truly a movie factory. The best of the "B"s are genuine art and the worst of the "B"s are genuine junk, but most of the "B"s do nothing more than epitomize the dictum that a movie is a movie, nothing more and nothing less.

1944 Industry Statistics

General

Theater Attendance

The average weekly attendance at motion picture theaters in the United States has been estimated by the MPPDA and industry executives at 95,000,000 on the basis of reports for the 52 weeks ending March 30, 1945.

United States Government tax collections indicate an average weekly paid attendance of approximately 81,500,000. This is based on a total admissions tax of $269,506,590 collected by the Bureau of Internal Revenue in the twelve months ending December 31, 1944. Motion picture theaters are unofficially credited with contributing 90.2% of the total amusement tax.

Weekly attendance, 1922–1943, estimated by MPPDA:

1922	40,000,000	1934	70,000,000
1923	43,000,000	1935	75,000,000
1924	46,000,000	1936	80,000,000
1925	48,000,000	1937	85,000,000
1926	50,000,000	1938	85,000,000
1927	57,000,000	1939	85,000,000
1928	65,000,000	1940	80,000,000
1929	95,000,000	1941	85,000,000
1930	110,000,000	1942	90,000,000
1931	75,000,000	1943	95,000,000
1932	60,000,000	1944	97,000,000
1933	60,000,000		

Number of Theaters and Seating Capacities

The latest records of the War Activities Committee list 16,500 theaters and other places of exhibition in the United States exhibiting motion pictures in operation as of December 31, 1944. About 2,500 closed

85

theaters are also reported. The last count, in 1939, by the Census Bureau of the U.S. Department of Commerce, showed 15,115 regularly operating motion picture theaters.

A *Motion Picture Herald* survey in February 1942 disclosed that 11 major distributors service 16,951 accounts in 8,488 cities, towns and villages in the United States. The accounts represent a total of 10,451,442 seats, one for every 12½ men, women and children counted in the 1940 census.

Because of wartime restrictions on building and remodeling there was very little change in the numerical strength of theaters during 1944.

The total of 16,951 now arrived at by compilation of distributor service accounts includes part-time resort theaters, occasional commercial showings in lodge and church halls and in other non-theatrical places. Army post theaters, drive-ins, so-called itinerants and closed theaters are excluded.

Seventy percent of the accounts are located in towns of less than 50,000 inhabitants and 86.5% of them seat less than 1,000 persons. The bulk of exhibition revenue, however, comes from 30% of the accounts in cities of more than 50,000 persons, where 46% of the seating capacity is concentrated.

The average seating capacity of all the accounts is 617. Indicative, however, of the concentration of seating capacity are the 2,374,108 seats in the 14 cities having more than 500,000 population. In these cities there are 2,301 accounts, only 12.9% of the total.

Exhibition Accounts in the U.S. by Seating Capacities

Seating Capacity	Number of Theaters		Cumulative Total	
	1941	1938	1941	1938
Over 3,000	112	117	– –	– –
2,000 to 3,000	319	374	431	491
1,500 to 2,000	556	689	987	1,180
1,000 to 1,500	1,312	1,646	2,299	2,826
500 to 1,000	4,689	5,500	6,988	8,326
200 to 500	7,854	7,303	14,842	15,629
200 and less	2,109	1,912	16,951	17,541

Exhibition Accounts in the U.S. by Location

The latest census showed that motion pictures were distributed in the United States in 1939 by 517 exchanges, of which 303 were producer-owned and 214 independently owned.

Total cost of all motion picture production in the United States, including feature pictures, short subjects, newsreels and non-theatrical pictures, was $215,664,929 in 1939, according to the Census Bureau. The increase since that year, owing principally to the costs added by wartime economy, is estimated by studio officials at 25%, bringing the average annual expenditure to $270,000,000.

Employment

Department of Commerce figures on employment in the industry are as follows:

	Average number per year	Payroll per year
Exhibition	145,600	$159,215,400
Distribution	14,300	44,741,300
Production:		
Stars, talent, salaried officers & employees	9,635	93,341,137
Wage earners	33,687	45,735,926
TOTALS	203,222	$343,033,763

Plant Investment

The capital investment is estimated by the Department of Commerce as:

Theaters	$1,900,000,000
Studios	125,000,000
Distribution	25,000,000
TOTAL	$2,050,000,000

Ticket Tax Collection

United States Treasury admission tax collections from places of amusement by months since November 1941, when the tax base was broadened to one cent for each ten cents of admission price are tabulated on p. 88. On April 1, 1944 the tax rate increased to one cent on each five cents, or major fraction thereof, of admission price.

Population of Towns	Towns with Theaters	Cumulative Total	No. of Theaters Operating	Cumulative Total	No. of Seats	Cumulative Total	Average Seats per Theater
Over 500,000	14	—	2,301	—	2,374,108	—	1,031
500,000 to 200,000	29	43	1,099	3,400	962,770	3,336,878	877
200,000 to 100,000	49	92	743	4,143	685,674	4,022,552	923
100,000 to 50,000	107	199	898	5,041	808,872	4,831,424	901
50,000 to 20,000	304	503	1,278	6,319	1,072,839	5,904,263	841
20,000 to 10,000	550	1,053	1,405	7,724	991,773	6,895,636	706
10,000 to 5,000	937	1,990	1,715	9,439	1,016,366	7,912,002	593
5,000 to 2,500	1,398	3,388	1,967	11,406	924,676	8,836,678	470
2,500 to 1,000	2,736	6,124	3,075	14,481	1,021,051	9,857,729	332
1,000 and less	2,364	8,488	2,470	16,951	613,713	10,451,442	248

Tax on box office receipts for month of	1942	Amount 1943	1944	1945
January	$ 9,769,398	$ 11,317,101	$ 10,582,411	$23,011,107
February	10,592,455	11,874,676	13,031,382	26,814,585
March	10,788,463	13,283,115	13,045,305	--
April	11,803,922	14,625,615	24,952,452	--
May	11,550,144	11,109,477	22,960,168	--
June	12,484,881	15,750,519	27,425,762	--
July	12,436,304	16,178,306	29,897,098	--
August	13,662,337	13,926,347	25,412,331	--
September	14,694,997	16,499,395	27,210,435	--
October	11,310,821	16,388,863	26,410,527	--
November	15,922,909	13,048,274	27,276,354	--
December	11,728,489	16,744,936	21,302,365	--
TOTAL	$146,745,120	$170,746,624	$269,506,590	--

Exhibition

General Economy

Reports of the Bureau of Census of the Department of Commerce show that the 15,115 theaters in operation in the United States in 1939 accounted for 33.7% of the total number of establishments coming within the scope of Places of Amusement; 67.4% of the total volume of business; 56.2% of the total employment, and 58.4% of the total payroll. The figures for the 1940 census, covering the year 1939, and for the last previous count, in 1935, compare as follows:

	1939	1935
Number of theaters	15,115	12,024
Receipts	$673,045,000	$508,196,000
Average number of employees	125,684	93,052
Total payroll	$131,583,000	$102,804,000

The MPPDA office estimates that the average motion picture theater, open about ten hours a day, takes in from 75 to 85% of its daily receipts between 7:30 and 8:30 p.m.

Double feature programs are shown in approximately 59% of all theaters — 30% every day and 29% part of the time. Average admission price is 27.5 cents, tax excluded.

Theater attendance by day of the week (Department of Commerce data): Monday, Tuesday, Wednesday and Thursday, 10%; Friday, 15%; Saturday, 20%; Sunday, 25%.

Theater Plant Construction and Replacement

New theaters (commercial indoor only) constructed from June 1941 to June 1942: 121.

Expenditures for new theater construction prior to mid-summer 1942 (when Government restrictions on theater construction came into full effect):

In 1929	$163,559,000
In 1930	97,580,000
In 1931 (approximated)	45,000,000
In 1932	17,500,000
In 1933	13,500,000
In 1934 to April 1935	20,000,000
In 1935 to April 1936	21,500,000
April 1936 to June 1937	46,275,000
June 1937 to June 1938	44,800,000
June 1938 to June 1939	38,300,000
June 1939 to June 1940	36,000,000
June 1940 to June 1941	27,800,000
June 1941 to June 1942	7,268,000

Estimated annual expenditure for theater equipment and supplies (new and replacement) in normal peacetime: $50,000,000

(Above data by Better Theatres)

Theater Operating Costs

Distribution of box office receipts is estimated by the MPPDA office as follows:

Theater retains 65% for local expenses as follows:
Payroll, staff and management	25%
Real estate: rent, insurance, taxes, interest and depreciation	15%
Local advertising and publicity	8%
Light and heat	5%
Interest and dividends.................	5%
Other taxes and insurance	4%
Extra attractions (acts, music, prizes, etc.).......................	3%

Theater pays 35% for film rental as follows:
To studios and production end	25%
To distributor for prints, advertising, sales and service costs, etc.............	10%

Theater Classifications

The MPPDA office estimated in 1941 that there were about 2,600 theaters operated by circuits affiliated with producer-distributor organizations, and that another 4,839 theaters are operated by 357 unaffiliated circuits. Other interesting figures:

Number of towns with motion picture theaters equipped for operation	8,488
Approximate number of first run theaters in 95 cities of over 100,000 population	450

Theaters usually showing first run pictures in the 400 largest cities of over 16,000 population:

90 towns have all first run theaters under independent operation	262 theaters
146 towns have all first run theaters under circuit management	415 theaters
164 towns have first run theaters under both circuit and independent management	683 theaters
Total first run independent theaters	522 with 641,533 seats
Maximum number of first run bookings possible in these cities on any one picture	400

Distribution

Exchange Operations

Motion picture film exchanges had gross receipts, principally from film rentals, of $243,482,000 in 1939, according to the latest census figures of the Department of Commerce. The total was an increase of 10.4% over the comparable total of $220,605,000 in 1929. The totals, divided between independent and producer exchanges, are as follows:

	Producer	Independent	Totals
No. of exchanges	303	214	517
Film rentals	$210,938,000	$32,544,000	$243,482,000
Operating expenses	$26,914,000	$6,925,000	$33,839,000
Employees	9,639	1,693	11,332
Payroll	$17,088,000	$4,107,000	$21,195,000

Total operating expenses (including payroll, but not cost of the films) was 13.9% of sales; payroll was 8.7% of sales.

Estimated number of film shipments per year between film exchanges and theaters.....................	15,000,000
Average number of positive prints required for each feature picture.....	200
Average number of newsreel prints for each issue....................	725
Average number of bookings per feature picture print..............	37
Average number of actual playing days per print	100
Average cost for each positive release print (feature length)	$200
General minimum bookings per picture	2,000
General maximum bookings per picture	12,000
Average screening per print..........	200

Exchange Centers

Albany	Milwaukee
Atlanta	Minneapolis
Boston	New Haven
Buffalo	New Orleans
Charlotte	New York
Chicago	Oklahoma City
Cincinnati	Omaha
Cleveland	Philadelphia
Dallas	Pittsburgh
Denver	Portland, Ore.
Des Moines	St. Louis
Detroit	Salt Lake City
Indianapolis	San Francisco
Kansas City	Seattle
Los Angeles	Washington
Memphis	

Production

Production Costs

According to the Census Bureau of the Department of Commerce, motion picture production of all types in the United States, measured by dollar cost, has increased approximately four-fold in twenty-five years. The annual production budget now exceeds $270,000,000 a year, compared with $77,000,000 in 1921; $86,000,000 in 1923; $93,000,000 in 1925; $184,000,000 in 1929; $197,000,000 in 1937; and $215,000,000 in 1939.

Production Cost Distribution

The average production budget is divided by the MPPDA, approximately as follows:

Cast.............................	25%
Extras, bits and characters	5%
Director	10%
Director assistants.................	2%
Cameraman and crew	1.5%
Lights	2%
Makeup, hairdressers and supplies	.9%
Teachers.........................	.2%
Crew and labor...................	1.2%
Story preparation	7%
Story costs	5%
Costumes and designers	2%
Sets and art directors	12.5%
Stills and photographs	.4%
Cutters	1%
Film negative.....................	1%
Tests	1.2%
Insurance	2%
Sound—Engineers and negatives	3.1%
Publicity, transportation, research, technical, miscellaneous...........	2%
Indirect costs	15%

Picture and Employment Facts

A total of 442 new features, of which 430 were domestic and 12 foreign, were approved in 1943 by the Production Code Administration. Other figures:

Number of different industries, arts and professions involved in the making of a feature	276
Total number of placements through Central Casting Bureau in 1944	325,000
Extras earned in 1944..............	$4,130,000

The following table shows a breakdown of the types and kinds of feature-length films released in 1944 as compared to 1943.

	1943	1944
Melodrama		
Action	18	26
Adventure	2	3
Comedy	9	21
Juvenile	8	6
Detective-Mystery	7	7
Murder-Mystery	22	33
Social Problem	18	7
Romantic	1	0
Fantasy	1	0
Spy Mystery	1	0
War	0	4
Musical	0	1
Psychological-Mystery	0	1
	87	109
Westerns		
Action	78	71
Mystery	1	10
Musical	4	4
	83	85
Drama		
Action	12	5
Biographical	8	5
Musical	4	8
Romantic	2	6
Social Problem	63	39
Comedy	1	9
Religious	1	3
Psychological	0	4
War	0	4
	91	83
Crime		
Action	2	5
Social Problem	5	0
Prison	0	0
	7	5

	1943	1944

Comedy

	1943	1944
Romantic	29	42
Musical	67	56
Juvenile	13	6
	109	104

Miscellaneous

	1943	1944
Farce-Murder Mystery	2	11
Farce-Comedy	9	20
Farce-Horror	0	1
Horror	16	13
Horror-Psychological	0	2
Cartoon	1	1
Documentary	5	4
Fantasy	2	1
Historical	1	1
Comedy-Fantasy	0	1
Travelogue	0	1
Sport	1	0
Romantic Musical	2	0
Musical	1	0
	40	56

TOTALS	417	442

The War Effort

Direct contributions to the war effort are made by the industry through the production or distribution, or both, of ten types of motion pictures: Victory Films (Government produced); America Speaks Films (industry produced); Films for Fighting Men; Army Training Films; Orientation Films; Strategy Films; Good Neighbor Films; Newsreels; Morale Films; United Nations Films.

Weekly war information releases by the Women's Army Corps consisted of twenty-six full-length short subjects and twenty-six Film Bulletins, on themes selected by the Office of War Information.

The industry to December 31, 1944 had contributed 24,867 16mm features, 26,341 16mm shorts to the overseas forces.

Allocation of Raw Stock
by War Production Board in Linear Feet

	1944 4th Qtr.	1945 1st Qtr.	1945 2nd Qtr.	1945 3rd Qtr.
Army	77,000,000	75,500,000	85,500,000	67,000,000
Navy	42,000,000	37,000,000	43,500,000	54,000,000
Canada	1,000,000	1,000,000	1,784,000	3,600,000
Foreign Economic Administration	50,000,000	66,835,000	52,000,000	38,000,000
Office of War Information				
Overseas	7,750,000	18,000,000	18,000,000	13,725,000
Domestic	5,000,000	8,300,000	17,250,000	8,750,000
Major entertainment picture producers	271,368,000	256,000,000	261,000,000	271,000,000
Newsreel producers	52,550,000	51,614,000	52,856,000	56,860,219
"Class C" producers	9,000,000	6,000,000	7,500,000	8,100,000
Factual picture producers	15,000,000	9,000,000	11,500,000	15,750,000
Special picture producers	3,000,000	1,500,000	5,500,000	6,300,000
Army & Navy Credits	58,000,000	60,000,000	66,000,000	74,100,000
Reserve	5,500,000	1,000,000	2,500,000	4,994,781
TOTALS	596,668,000	600,749,000	624,890,000	622,180,000

Raw Stock for Independent Production:
April, 1945 to April, 1946

Linear Feet

Group I

Walt Disney Productions	12,000,000
Samuel Goldwyn.	12,500,000
Sol Lesser	7,000,000
Edward Small	10,650,000
Harry Sherman	11,150,000
Eagle-Lion Films, Inc. (Rank)	5,200,000

Linear Feet

Group II

Edward A. Golden	3,000,000
Charles R. Rogers	6,000,000
Benedict Bogeaus	3,450,000
Walter Colmes	3,200,000
International Pictures, Inc.	15,000,000
Andrew Stone	3,000,000
Lester Cowan	4,000,000
Cagney Productions, Inc.	4,000,000
David Selznick (Vanguard Films)	15,000,000
Hunt Stromberg	5,150,000
Seymour Nebenzal	3,500,000
Jack Skirball	7,600,000
Arnold Productions, Inc.	4,150,000

Group III

Constance Bennett	2,575,000
Charles House	920,000
Howard Hughes	5,787,000
Jules Levey	4,000,000
David Loew	4,000,000
Morey & Sutherland Productions	848,000
Mary Pickford	5,000,000
Producers Corporation of America	3,400,000
Ripley Monter Productions	1,375,000
William Rowland Productions	1,432,000
William Wilder	1,140,000

TOTAL FOOTAGE 166,027,000

Checklist of PRC Films

Accomplice. © 1946. 7 reels, sd., 35mm. (R) September 29, 1946. 68 mins. *With* Richard Arlen, Veda Ann Borg. *Producer* John K. Teaford *Director* Walter Colmes *Screenplay* Irving Elman, Frank Gruber *Music* Alexander Laszlo *Photographer* Jockey Feindel *Film Editor* Robert Jahns. From the novel *Simon Lash, Private Detective* by Frank Gruberg. *Appl. author* PRC Pictures, Inc. © Pathe Industries, Inc., 12 September 1946; LP507.

Along the Sundown Trail. (R) October 1, 1942. *With* Bill "Cowboy Rambler" Boyd, Art Davis, Lee Powell, Julie Duncan, Kermit Maynard, Charles King, Howard Masters, Karl Hackett, John Merton, Jack Ingram, Ted Adams, Herman Hack, Frank Ellis, Jack Holmes, Reed Howes, Al St. John, Augie Gomez, Art Dillard, Al Taylor, Tex Palmer, Curley Dresden, Steve Clark, Hal Price, Jimmy Aubrey, Roy Bucko, Buck Bucko. *Producer* Sigmund Neufeld *Director* Peter Stewart (Sam Newfield) *Screenplay* Arthur St. Claire *Music* Johnny Lange, Lew Porter *Film Editor* Holbrook N. Todd.

Amazing Mr. Forrest. (R) March 29, 1944. 71 mins. *With* Edward Everett Horton, Jack Buchanan.

Ambush Trail. © 1946. 6 reels, sd. (R) February 17, 1946. 60 mins. *With* Bob Steele, Syd Saylor, Lorraine Miller, I. Stanford Jolley, Charles King, Bob Cason, Budd Buster, Kermit Maynard, Frank Ellis, Edward Cassidy, Roy Brent. *Producer* Arthur Alexander *Director* Harry Fraser *Screenplay* Elmer Clifton *Music Director* Lee Zahler. *Appl. Author* PRC Pictures, Inc. © Pathe Industries, Inc., 21 June 1946; LP411.

Apology for Murder. © 1945. 7 reels, sd. (R) September 27, 1945. 67 mins. *With* Ann Savage, Hugh Beaumont. *Producer* Sigmund Neufeld *Director* Sam

---

This list does not include many British or domestic "pickups" distributed by PRC, nor does it include re-issues and re-edits (PRC later edited many of their westerns down to 38–40 minute four-reel "Streamliners," for example, and these are not listed here), as well as such films as Brute Man, *made at Universal but sold to PRC, or* Hitler's Madman, *made for PRC but sold to MGM. It includes Eagle-Lion/PRC films through 1947, but ends at Dec. 31, 1947, by which time Eagle Lion had completely absorbed PRC.*

The following abbreviations have been used in this checklist: (R) — release date; sd. — sound; b&w — black and white.

Edward Everett Horton (left) gets a pointer from Jack Buchanan in "Amazing Mr. Forrest."

Newfield *Original story and screenplay* Fred Myton *Music Director* Leo Erdody *Film Editor* Holbrook N. Todd.
© PRC Pictures, Inc., 27 September 1945; LP13574.

Arizona Gang Busters. ©1940. 6 reels, sd. (R) September 16, 1940. 60 mins. *With* Tim McCoy, Pauline Haddon, Lou Fulton, Forrest Taylor, Julian Rivero, Arno Frey, Kenne Duncan, Jack Rutherford, Elizabeth LaMal, Otto Reichow, Lita Cortez, Carl Mathews, Ben Corbett, Frank Ellis, Curly Dresden. *Producer* Sigmund Neufeld *Director* Peter Stewart (Sam Newfield) *Original Screenplay* William Lively *Music Director* Lew Porter *Film Editor* Holbrook N. Todd.
© PRC Pictures, Inc., 11 September 1940; LP9906.

Arson Squad. Alexander-Stern, © 1945. 7 reels, sd. (R) September 11, 1945. 66 mins. Presented by PRC Pictures, Inc. *With* Frank Albertson, Robert Armstrong. *Producer* Arthur Alexander *Director* Lew Landers *Original Screenplay* Arthur St. Claire *Music Director* Lee Zahler *Film Editor* Holbrook N. Todd.
© PRC Pictures, Inc., 11 September 1945; LP13609.

Avalanche. © 1946. 8 reels, sd. 35mm. (R) June 20, 1946. 70 mins. Presented by PRC Pictures, Inc. An Imperial production. *With* Bruce Cabot, Roscoe Karns. *Producer* Pat de Cicco *Director* Irving Allen *Original Screenplay* Andrew Holt *Original Music Score* Lucien Moraweck, Rene Garriguenc *Music Director* Lud Gluskin *Film Editor* Louis Sackin. *Appl. Author* PRC Pictures, Inc.
© Pathe Industries, Inc., 20 June 1946; LP443.

Baby Face Morgan. © 1942. 7 reels, sd. (R) September 15, 1942. 62 mins. *With* Mary Carlisle, Richard Cromwell. *Producer* Jack Schwarz *Director* Arthur Dreifuss *Story* Oscar Brodney, Jack Rubin *Screenplay* Edward Dein, Jack Rubin *Original Music Score* Leo Erdody *Film Editor* Dan Milner.
© Producers Releasing Corp., 11 September 1942; LP11583.

Bad Men of Thunder Gap. © 1943. 6 reels, sd. (R) March 5, 1943. 57 mins. ("Texas Rangers" series) *With* Dave "Tex" O'Brien, Jim Newill, Guy Wilkerson, Janet Shaw, Jack Ingram, Charles King, Michael Vallon, Lucille Vance, Tom London, I. Stanford Jolley, Bud Osborne, Jimmy Aubrey, Artie Ortego, Cal Shrum and his Rhythm Rangers (Robert Hoag, Don Weston, Rusty Cline, Art Wenzel). *Producers* Alfred Stern, Arthur Alexander *Director* Albert Herman *Original Story and Screenplay* Elmer Clifton *Music Director* Lee Zahler *Cameraman* Robert Cline *Film Editor* Charles Henkel, Jr.
© Producers Releasing Corp., 20 February 1943; LP11872.

Beasts of Berlin (Goose Step, Hell's Devils). (R) October 29, 1939. 84 mins. *With* Roland Drew, Steffi Duna, Alan Ladd. *Director* Sam Newfield.

Behind Prison Walls. © 1943. 7 reels, sd. (R) March 22, 1943. 64 mins. *With* Alan Baxter, Gertrude Michael, Tully Marshall, Edwin Maxwell, Jacqueline Dalya, Matt Willis, Richard King, Alga Sabin, Isabelle Withers, Lane Chandler, Paul Everton, George Guhl, Regina Wallace. *Producer* Arthur Ripley *Director* Steve Sekely *Screenplay* Van Norcross *Music Director* David Chudnow *Film Editor* Holbrook N. Todd *Associate Producer* Andre Dumonceau *Cameraman* Marcel Le Picard. Based on an original story by W.A. Ullman, Jr.
© Producers Releasing Corp.; 3 March 1943; LP11887.

The Big Fix. © 1947. sd., b&w, 35mm. (R) April 19, 1946. 63 mins. *With* James Brown, Sheila Ryan, Noreen Nash, Regis Toomey. *Associate producer* Marvin D. Stahl *Director* James Flood *Screenplay* George Bricker, Aubrey Wisberg *Adaptation* Joel Malone *Music* Emil Cadkin *Music Director* Irving Friedman *Film Editor* Norman Colbert. Based on an original story by Sonia Chernus and George Ross.
© Pathe Industries, Inc.; 19 April 1947; LP960.

Billy the Kid in "Blazing Frontier." © 1943. 6 reels, sd. (R) September 1, 1943. 59 mins. ("Billy the Kid" series.) *With* Buster Crabbe, Al St. John, Marjorie Manners, Milt Kibbee, I. Stanford Jolley, Kermit Maynard, Frank Hagney, George Chesebro, Frank Ellis, Hank Bell, Jimmy Aubrey. *Producer* Sigmund Neufeld *Director* Sam Newfield *Original Story and Screenplay* Patricia Harper *Film Editor* Holbrook N. Todd.
© Producers Releasing Corp., 21 August 1943; LP12205.

Billy the Kid in "Cattle Stampede." (R) August 16, 1943. 58 mins. ("Billy the Kid" series.) *With* Buster Crabbe, Al St. John, Frances Gladwin, Charles King, Ed Cassidy, Hansel Warner, Ray Bennett, Frank Ellis, Steve Clark, Roy Brent, John Elliott, Budd Buster, Hank Bell, Tex Cooper, Ted Adams, Frank McCarroll, Ray Jones, Rose Plummer, George Morrell. *Producer* Sigmund Neufeld *Director* Sam Newfield *Screenplay* Joseph O'Donnell *Film Editor* Holbrook N. Todd.

Billy the Kid in "Fugitive of the Plains." (R) March 12, 1943. 56 mins. ("Billy the Kid" series.) *With* Buster Crabbe, Al St. John, Maxine Leslie, Kermit Maynard, Jack Ingram, Karl Hackett, Hal Price, Budd Buster, Artie Ortego, Carl Sepulveda. *Producer* Sigmund Neufeld *Director* Sam Newfield *Screenplay*

George Sayre *Music* Leo Erdody *Film Editor* Holbrook N. Todd *Cameraman* Jack Greenhalgh.
© Producers Releasing Corp.; 2 March 1943; LP11886.

Billy the Kid in "Law and Order." © 1943. 6 reels, sd. (R) August 21, 1942. 58 mins. ("Billy the Kid" series.) *With* Buster Crabbe, Al St. John, Tex (Dave) O'Brien, Sarah Padden, Wanda McKay, Charles King, Hal Price, John Merton, Kenne Duncan, Ted Adams, Budd Buster, Kermit Maynard. *Producer* Sigmund Neufeld *Director* Sherman Scott (Sam Newfield) *Original Screenplay* Sam Robins *Film Editor* Holbrook N. Todd.
© Producers Releasing Corp.; 5 February 1943; LP11836.

Billy the Kid in Santa Fe. ©1941. 5 reels, sd. (R) July 11, 1941. 66 mins. ("Billy the Kid" series.) *With* Bob Steele, Al St. John, Rex Lease, Marin Sais, Dennis Moore, Karl Hackett, Steve Clark, Hal Price, Charles King, Frank Ellis, Dave O'Brien, Kenne Duncan, Curley Dresden. *Producer* Sigmund Neufeld *Director* Sherman Scott (Sam Newfield) *Original Screenplay* Joseph O'Donnell *Music* Johnny Lange, Lew Porter *Film Editor* Holbrook N. Todd.
© Producers Releasing Corp., 3 July 1941; LP10580.

Billy the Kid in Texas. © 1940. 6 reels, sd. (R) September 30, 1940. 63 mins. ("Billy the Kid" series.) *With* Bob Steele, Al St. John, Terry Walker, Carleton Young, Charles King, John Merton, Frank LaRue, Slim Whitaker, Curley Dresden, Tex Palmer, Chick Hannon, Merrill McCormack, Denver Dixon, Bob Woodward, Sherry Tansey, Herman Hack, Pasquel Perry. *Producer* Sigmund Neufeld *Director* Peter Stewart (Sam Newfield) *Original Screenplay* Joseph O'Donnell *Music Director* Lew Porter *Film Editor* Holbrook N. Todd.
© Producers Releasing Corp.; 30 September 1940; LP9940.

Billy the Kid in "The Kid Rides Again." (R) January 27, 1943. 60 mins. ("Billy the Kid" series.) *With* Buster Crabbe, Al St. John, Iris Meredith, Glenn Strange, Charles King, I. Stanford Jolley, Edward Piel, Ted Adams, Karl Hackett, Kenne Duncan, Curley Dresden, Snub Pollard, John Merton, Slim Whitaker. *Producer* Sigmund Neufeld *Director* Sherman Scott *Screenplay* Fred Myton.

Billy the Kid in "The Mysterious Rider." © 1943. 6 reels, sd. (R) November 20, 1943. 55 mins. ("Billy the Kid" series.) *With* Buster Crabbe, Al St. John, Caroline Burke, John Merton, Kermit Maynard, Jack Ingram, Slim Whitaker, Ted Adams, Guy Wilkerson, Edwin Brien, Frank Ellis. *Producer* Sigmund Neufeld *Director* Sherman Scott (Sam Newfield) *Screenplay* Steve Braxton (Sam Robins) *Cameraman* Jack Greenhalgh *Film Editor* Holbrook N. Todd.
© PRC Pictures, Inc., 1 July 1943; LP13612.

Billy the Kid in "The Renegades." © 1943. 6 reels, sd. (R) July 1, 1943. 58 mins. ("Billy the Kid" series.) *With* Buster Crabbe, Al St. John, Lois Ranson, Karl Hackett, Ray Bennett, Frank Hagney, Jack Rockwell, Tom Londôn, George Chesebro, Jimmy Aubrey, Carl Sepulveda, Dan White, Wally West. *Producer* Sigmund Neufeld *Director* Sam Newfield, David Chudnow *Cameraman* Robert Cline *Film Editor* Holbrook N. Todd *Original Story* George Milton (George Sayre, Milton Raison) *Screenplay* Joseph O'Donnell.
© PRC Pictures, Inc., 1 July 1943; LP13612.

Billy the Kid in "Western Cyclone." © 1943. 6 reels, sd. (R) May 14, 1943. 56 mins. ("Billy the Kid" series.) *With* Buster Crabbe, Al St. John, Marjorie Manners, Karl Hackett. *Producer* Sigmund Neufeld *Director* Sam Newfield *Screenplay* Patricia Harper *Music* Leo Erdody *Film Editor* Holbrook N. Todd. © Producers Releasing Corp., 10 May 1943; LP12055.

Billy the Kid Outlawed. © 1940. 6 reels, sd. (R) July 20, 1940. 52 mins. ("Billy the Kid" series.) *With* Bob Steele, Al St. John, Louise Currie, Carleton Young, John Merton, Joe McGuinn, Ted Adams, Walter McGrail, Hal Price, Kenne Duncan, Reed Howes, George Chesebro, Steve Clark, Budd Buster. *Producer* Sigmund Neufeld *Director* Peter Stewart (Sam Newfield) *Screenplay* Oliver Drake.

Billy the Kid Trapped. © 1942. 6 reels, sd. (R) February 20, 1942. 59 mins. ("Billy the Kid" series.) *With* Buster Crabbe, Al St. John, Bud McTaggart, Anne Jeffries, Glenn Strange, Walter McGrail, Ted Adams, Jack Ingram, Milt Kibbee, Eddie Phillips, Budd Buster, Jack Kinney, Jimmy Aubrey, Wally West, Bert Dillard, Kenne Duncan, George Chesebro, Carl Mathews, Dick Cramer, Ray Henderson, Curley Dresden, Augie Gomez, Horace B. Carpenter, Herman Hack, James Mason, Hank Bell, Oscar Gahan. *Producer* Sigmund Neufeld *Director* Sherman Scott (Sam Newfield) *Original Screenplay* Joseph O'Donnell *Music* Johnny Lange, Lew Porter *Film Editor* Holbrook N. Todd. © Producers Releasing Corp., 30 January 1942; LP11053.

Billy the Kid Wanted. © 1941. 6 reels, sd. (R) October 24, 1941. 64 mins. ("Billy the Kid" series.) *With* Buster Crabbe, Al St. John, Dave O'Brien, Glenn Strange, Choti Sherwood, Charles King, Slim Whitaker, Howard Masters, Joe Newfield, Budd Buster, Frank Ellis, Curley Dresden, Wally West. *Producer* Sigmund Neufeld *Director* Sherman Scott (Sam Newfield) *Original Screenplay* Fred Myton *Music* Johnny Lange, Lew Porter *Film Editor* Holbrook N. Todd. © Producers Releasing Corp., 4 October 1941; LP10758.

Billy the Kid's Fighting Pals. © 1941. 6 reels, sd. (R) April 18, 1941. 62 mins. ("Billy the Kid" series.) *With* Bob Steele, Al St. John, Phyllis Adair, Carleton Young, Charles King, Curley Dresden, Edward Piel, Sr., Hal Price, George Chesebro, Forrest Taylor, Budd Buster, Julian Rivero, Ray Henderson, Wally West, Art Dillard. *Producer* Sigmund Neufeld *Director* Sherman Scott (Sam Newfield) *Story* George Plympton *Music Director* Dave Chudnow *Film Editor* Holbrook N. Todd. © Producers Releasing Corp., 9 April 1941; LP10391.

Billy the Kid's Gun Justice. © 1940. 6 reels, sd. (R) December 27, 1940. 63 mins. ("Billy the Kid" series.) *With* Bob Steele, Al St. John, Louise Currie, Carleton Young, Charles King, Rex Lease, Ted Adams, Kenne Duncan, Forrest Taylor, Al Ferguson, Karl Hackett, Edward Piel, Sr., Julian Rivero, Blanca Vischer. *Producer* Sigmund Neufeld *Director* Peter Stewart (Sam Newfield) *Original Screenplay* Tom Gibson *Music Director* Lew Porter *Film Editor* Holbrook N. Todd. © Producers Releasing Corp., 25 December 1940; LP10151.

Billy the Kid's Range War. © 1941. 6 reels, sd. (R) January 24, 1941. 60 mins. ("Billy the Kid" series.) *With* Bob Steele, Al St. John, Joan Barclay, Carleton

Young, Rex Lease, Buddy Roosevelt, Milt Kibbee, Karl Hackett, Ted Adams, Julian Rivero, John Ince, Alden Chase, Howard Masters, Ralph Peters, Charles King, George Chesebro, Steve Clark, Tex Palmer. *Producer* Sigmund Neufeld *Director* Peter Stewart (Sam Newfield) *Original Screenplay* William Lively *Music Director* Lew Porter *Film Editor* Holbrook N. Todd.
© Producers Releasing Corp., 16 January 1941; LP10171.

Billy the Kid's Roundup. © 1941. 6 reels, sd. (R) December 12, 1941. 58 mins. ("Billy the Kid" series.) *With* Buster Crabbe, Al St. John, Carleton Young, Joan Barclay, Glenn Strange, Charles King, Slim Whitaker, John Elliott, Dennis Moore, Kenne Duncan, Curley Dresden, Dick Cramer, Wally West, Tex Palmer, Tex Cooper, Horace B. Carpenter, Jim Mason. *Producer* Sigmund Neufeld *Director* Sherman Scott (Sam Newfield) *Original Screenplay* Fred Myton *Music* Johnny Lange, Lew Porter *Film Editor* Holbrook N. Todd.
© Producers Releasing Corp., 14 November 1941; LP10823.

Billy the Kid's Smoking Guns. © 1942. 6 reels, sd. (R) May 29, 1942. 58 mins. ("Billy the Kid" series.) *With* Buster Crabbe, Al St. John, Dave O'Brien, Joan Barclay, John Merton, Milt Kibbee, Ted Adams, Karl Hackett, Frank Ellis, Slim Whitaker, Budd Buster, Joel Newfield, Bert Dillard. *Producer* Sigmund Neufeld *Director* Sherman Scott (Sam Newfield) *Original Screenplay* George Milton (George Sayre, Milton Raison) *Music* Johnny Lange, Lew Porter *Film Editor* Holbrook N. Todd.
© Producers Releasing Corp., 21 May 1942; LP11321.

The Black Raven. © 1943. 6 reels, sd. (R) May 31, 1943. 61 mins. *With* George Zucco, Wanda McKay, Noel Madison, Bob Randall, Byron Foulger, Charlie Middleton, Robert Middlemass, Glenn Strange, I. Stanford Jolley. *Producer* Sigmund Neufeld *Director* Sam Newfield *Original Screenplay* Fred Myton *Film Editor* Holbrook N. Todd *Musical Supervisor* David Chudnow *Cameraman* Robert Cline.
© Producers Releasing Corp., 19 April 1943; LP11993.

Blazing Frontier. See **Billy the Kid in "Blazing Frontier."**

Blonde for a Day. © 1946. 7 reels, sd., 35 mm. (R) August 29, 1946. 68 mins. Presented by PRC Pictures, Inc. *With* Hugh Beaumont, Kathryn Adams. *Producer* Sigmund Neufeld *Director* Sam Newfield *Screenplay* Fred Myton *Music Director* Leo Erdody *Film Editor* Holbrook N. Todd. Based upon original characters and story by Brett Halliday.
© Pathe Industries, Inc., 6 July 1946; LP454.

Bluebeard. © 1944. 8 reels, sd. (R) November 11, 1944. 73 mins. *With* John Carradine, Jean Parker. *Producer* Leon Fromkess *Director* Edgar G. Ulmer *Original Story* Arnold Phillips, Werner H. Furst *Screenplay* Pierre Gendron *Photography* Jockey A. Feindel (Eugen Schüftan).
© PRC Pictures, Inc., 12 November 1944; LP13562.

Bombs Over Burma. © 1942. 7 reels, sd. (R) June 5, 1942. 65 mins. *With* Anna May Wong, Noel Madison. *Producers* Alfred Stern, Arthur Alexander *Director* Joseph H. Lewis *Original Screenplay* Milton Raison, Joseph H. Lewis

The blind man turns out to be an assassin in this scene from "Dawn Express" (retitled "Nazi Spy Ring"). As is the case with many PRC films, none of these apparently significant characters were listed in the credits, making this a truly anonymous murder.

Music Direction Lee Zahler *Photographer* Robert Cline *Film Editor* Charles Henkel, Jr.
© Producers Releasing Corp., 28 May 1942; LP11341.

Border Badmen. © 1945. 6 reels, sd. (R) October 10, 1945. 59 mins. ("Billy Carson" series) *With* Buster Crabbe, Al St. John, Lorraine Miller, Charles King, Ray Bennett, Archie Hall, Budd Buster, Marilyn Gladstone, Marin Sais, Bud Osborne, Bob Kortman. *Producer* Sigmund Neufeld *Director* Sam Newfield *Original Story and Screenplay* George Milton *Music Director* Frank Sanucci *Film Editor* Holbrook N. Todd.
© PRC Pictures, Inc., 10 October 1945; LP13575.

Border Buckaroos. © 1943. 6 reels, sd. (R) June 15, 1943. 59 mins. ("Texas Rangers" series.) *With* Dave O'Brien, Jim Newill, Guy Wilkerson, Christine McIntyre, Eleanor Counts, Jack Ingram, Ethan Laidlaw, Charles King, Michael Vallon, Kenne Duncan, Reed Howes, Kermit Maynard, Bud Osborne. *Producers* Alfred Stern, Arthur Alexander *Director* Oliver Drake *Author* Oliver Drake *Screenplay* Oliver Drake *Musical Director* Lee Zahler *Art Director* Fred Preble *Songs* Dave O'Brien, Jim Newill *Cameraman* Ira Morgan *Film Editor* Charles Henkel, Jr.
© Producers Releasing Corp., 16 June 1943; LP12097.

Border Feud. © 1947. (R) May 10, 1947. 55 mins., sd., b&w, 35mm. *With* Lash La Rue, Al St. John, Gloria Marlen, Bob Duncan, Brad Slaven, Kenneth Farrell, Casey MacGregor, Mikel Conrad, Ed Cassidy, Ian Keith, Bud Osborne, Frank Ellis, Dick Cramer. *Producer* Jerry Thomas *Director* Ray Taylor *Screenplay* Joseph O'Donnell, Patricia Harper *Film Editor* Joe Gluck.
© Pathe Industries, Inc., 10 May 1947; LP1028.

Border Roundup. © 1943. 6 reels, sd. (R) September 18, 1942. ("Lone Rider" series.) *With* George Houston, Al St. John, Dennis Moore, Patricia Knox, John Elliott, Charles King, I. Stanford Jolley, Edward Piel, Sr., Jimmy Aubrey, Dale Sherwood, Nick Thompson, Frank Ellis, Curley Dresden, Lynton Brent. *Producer* Sigmund Neufeld *Director* Sam Newfield *Screenplay* Steven Worth *Music* Johnny Lange *Film Editor* Holbrook N. Todd.
© Producers Releasing Corp., 10 February 1943; LP11853.

Born to Speed. © 1947. sd., b&w, 35 mm. (R) January 12, 1947. 61 mins. *With* Johnny Sands, Terry Austin. *Producer* Ben Stoloff *Director* Edward L. Cahn *Screenplay* Crane Wilbur, Scott Darling, Robert B. Churchill *Music* Albert Levin *Music Director* Irving Friedman *Film Editor* W. Donn Hayes. Based on an original story by Robert B. Churchill.
© Pathe Industries, Inc., 12 January 1947; LP830.

The Boss of Big Town. © 1942. 7 reels, sd. (R) December 7, 1942. 64 mins. *With* John Litel, Florence Rice. *Producer* Jack Schwartz *Director* Arthur Dreifuss *Original Story* Arthur Hoerl *Screenplay* Edward Dein *Music Director* Leo Erdody *Film Editor* Charles Henkel, Jr.
© Producers Releasing Corp., 4 November 1942; LP11683.

Boss of Rawhide. © 1943. 6 reels, sd. (R) November 20, 1943. 59 mins. ("Texas Ranger" series.) *With* Dave O'Brien, Jim Newill, Guy Wilkerson, Nell O'Day, Edward Cassidy, Jack Ingram, Billy Bletcher, Charles King, George Chesebro, Robert Hill, Dan White, Lucille Vance, Bob Kortman. *Producer* Alfred Stern *Director and Screenplay* Elmer Clifton *Music Director* Lee Zahler *Photographer* Robert Cline *Film Editor* Charles Henkel, Jr.
© PRC Pictures, Inc., 20 November 1943; LP12373.

Brand of the Devil. © 1944. 6 reels, sd. (R) July 30, 1944. 57 mins. ("Texas Rangers" series) *With* Dave O'Brien, Jim Newill, Guy Wilkerson, Ellen Hall, I. Stanford Jolley, Charles King, Reed Howes, Kermit Maynard, Budd Buster, Karl Hackett, Ed Cassidy. *Producer* Arthur Alexander *Director* Harry Fraser *Original Screenplay* Elmer Clifton *Music Director* Lee Zahler *Photographer* Edward Kull *Film Editor* Charles Henkel, Jr.
© PRC Pictures, Inc., 15 July 1944; LP12736.

Broadway Big Shot. © 1942. 7 reels, sd. (R) February 6, 1942. 59 mins. *With* Ralph Byrd, Virginia Vale. *Producer* Jed Buell *Director* William Beaudine *Original Story and Screenplay* Martin Mooney *Film Editor* Guy Thayer, Jr.
© Producers Releasing Corp., 28 January 1942; LP11054.

Buried Alive. (R) November 6, 1939. 62 mins. Producers Distributing Corp. *With* Beverly Roberts, Robert Wilcox.

The Caravan Trail. © 1946. 7 reels, sd., color (Cinecolor). (R) April 20, 1946. 57 mins. *With* Eddie Dean, Emmett Lynn, Al "Lash" LaRue, Jean Carlin, Robert Malcolm, Charles King, Robert Barron, Forrest Taylor, Bob Duncan, Jack O'Shea, Terry Frost, George Chesebro, Bud Osborne, Lee Roberts, Wylie Grant, Lee Bennett, Lloyd Ingraham. *Director* Robert Emmett (Tansey) *Original Screenplay* Frances Kavanaugh *Musical Director* Carl Hoefle.
© PRC Pictures, Inc., 22 June 1946; LP412.

Career Girl. © 1943. 7 reels, sd. (R) January 11, 1944. 69 mins. *With* Frances Langford, Craig Wood, Edward Norris, Iris Adrian, Linda Brent, Alec Craig, Ariel Heath, Lorraine Krueger, Renee White, Gladys Blake, Charles Judels, Charles Williams. *Producer* Jack Schwarz *Associate Producer* Harry D. Edwards *Director* Wallace W. Fox *Authors* Dave Silverstein, Stanley Rauh *Screenplay* Sam Neuman *Art Director* Paul Sylos *Musical Director* Rudy Schrager *Musical Supervisor* David Chudnow *Cameraman* Gustave Peterson *Film Editor* Robert Crandall.
© PRC Pictures, Inc., 11 January 1944; LP12426.

Castle of Crimes. © 1944. 6 reels, sd. (R) August 25, 1944. 60 mins. (PRC British pickup) *With* Kenneth Kent, Diana Churchill. *Producer* A.E.W. Mason *Director* Harold French *Scenario* Doreen Montgomery *Photography* Walter Harvey *Film Editor* E.B. Jarves.
© PRC Pictures, Inc., 15 December 1944; LP13009.

Cattle Stampede. See **Billy the Kid in "Cattle Stampede."**

Caught in the Act. © 1941. 7 reels, sd. (R) January 17, 1941. 62 mins. *With* Henry Armetta. *Producer* T.H. Richmond *Director* Jean Yarbrough *Original Story* Robert Cosgriff *Screenplay* Al Martin.
© Producers Releasing Corp., 25 January 1941; LP10209.

Cheyenne. See **The Lone Rider in "Cheyenne."**

Cheyenne Takes Over. © 1947. sd., 35 mm., b&w. (R) December 13, 1947. 58 mins. New PRC Pictures, Inc. *With* "Lash" La Rue, Al St. John, Nancy Gates, George Chesebro, Lee Morgan, John Merton, Steve Clark, Bob Woodward, Marshall Reed, Budd Buster, Carl Mathews, Dee Cooper, Brad Slaven, Hank Bell. *Producer* Jerry Thomas *Director* Ray Taylor *Screenplay* Arthur E. Orloff *Music* Walter Greene *Film Editor* Joe Gluck.
© Pathe Industries, Inc., 25 October 1947; LP1309.

City of Silent Men. © 1942. 7 reels, sd. (R) October 12, 1942. 64 mins. *With* Frank Albertson, June Lang. *Producer* Dixon R. Harwin *Director* William Nigh *Screenplay* Joseph Hoffman *Music Score* Leo Erdody *Music Direction* David Chudnow *Film Editor* Carl Pierson. From an original story by Robert E. Kent and Joseph Hoffman.
© Producers Releasing Corp., 8 October 1942; LP11680.

Club Havana. © 1945. 6 reels, sd. (R) November 23, 1945. 62 mins. *With* Tom Neal, Margaret Lindsay. *Director* Edgar G. Ulmer *Original Story* Fred L. Jackson *Screenplay* Raymond L. Schrock *Cameraman* Eugen Schüftan.
© PRC Pictures, Inc., 5 November 1945; LP13581.

Otto Kruger (center, white shirt) faces impossible odds in this scene from "Corregidor." Donald Woods (extreme right) and Elissa Landi (second from left) assist him in his front-line surgical practice.

Colorado Serenade. © 1946. 7 reels, color (Cinecolor). (R) June 30, 1946. 68 mins. With Eddie Dean, Roscoe Ates, David Sharpe, Mary Kenyon, Forrest Taylor, Dennis Moore, Abigail Adams, Warner Richmond, Lee Bennett, Robert McKenzie, Bob Duncan, Charles King, Bud Osborne. Director Robert Emmett Tansey Original Screenplay Frances Kavanaugh. Appl. author PRC Pictures, Inc.
© Pathe Industries, Inc., 19 June 1946; LP410.

The Contender. © 1944. 7 reels, sd. (R) May 10, 1944. 66 mins. With Buster Crabbe, Arline Judge. Producer Bert Sternbach Director Sam Newfield Original Story George Sayre, Jay Doten Screenplay George Sayre, Jay Doten, Raymond Schrock Music Score Albert Glasser Film Editor Holbrook N. Todd.
© PRC Pictures, Inc., 10 May 1944; LP12654.

Corregidor. © 1943. 8 reels, sd. (R) March 29, 1943. 73 mins. With Otto Kruger, Elissa Landi, Donald Woods, Frank Jenks, Rick Vallin, Wanda McKay, Ian Keith, Ted Hecht, Charles Jordan, Frank Jacquet, I. Stanford Jolley, John Grant, Ruby Dandridge, Forrest Taylor, Jack Rutherford, Eddie Hall. Producers Dixon R. Harwin, Edward Finney Director William Nigh Original Story and Screenplay Doris Malloy, Edgar Ulmer Music Leo Erdody Photography Ira

C. Morgan *Film Editor* Charles Henkel, Jr. *Musical Supervisor* David Chudnow *Art Director* F. Paul Sylos.

Crime, Inc. © 1945. 8 reels, sd. (R) April 15, 1945. 75 mins. *With* Leo Carrillo, Tom Neal. *Producer* Leon Fromkess *Director* Lew Landers *Screenplay* Ray Schrock *Music* Walter Greene *Film Editor* Roy Livingston. From the book by Martin Mooney.
© PRC Pictures, Inc., 16 March 1945; LP13171.

Criminals Within. © 1941. 7 reels, sd. (R) June 27, 1941. 70 mins. *With* Eric Linden, Ann Doran. *Producer* E.B. Derr *Director* Joseph Lewis *Original Story* Arthur Hoerl *Screenplay* Edward Bennett *Photography* Arthur Martinelli *Film Editor* Howard Dillinger.
© Producers Releasing Corp., 13 June 1941; LP10533.

Danger! Women at Work. © 1943. 6 reels, sd. (R) August 23, 1943. 59 mins. *With* Patsy Kelly, Mary Brian, Isabel Jewell, Wanda McKay, Betty Compson, Cobina Wright, Sr., Allan Byron, Warren Hymer, Michael Kirk, Vince Barnett. *Producer* Jack Schwarz *Associate Producer* Harry D. Edwards *Director* Sam Newfield *Authors* Gertrude Walker, Edgar G. Ulmer *Screenplay* Martin Mooney *Art Director* Frank Sylos *Cameraman* Ira Morgan *Editor* Robert O. Crandall.
© PRC Pictures, Inc., 23 August 1943; LP13571.

Dangerous Intruder. © 1945. 7 reels, sd. (R) September 21, 1945. 65 mins. *With* Charles Arnt, Veda Ann Borg. *Director* Vernon Keays *Original Story* Philip MacDonald, F. Ruth Howard *Music* Karl Hajos.
PRC Pictures, Inc., 21 November 1945; LP416.

Dangerous Lady. © 1941. 6 reels, sd. (R) September 12, 1941. 60 mins. *With* Neil Hamilton, June Storey. *Producer and Director* Bernard B. Ray *Original Story* Leslie T. White *Screenplay* Jack Natteford *Music Director* Clarence Wheeler *Film Editor* Carl Himm.
© Producers Releasing Corp., 18 September 1941; LP10764.

Danny Boy. © 1946. Presented by PRC Pictures, Inc. 7 reels, sd., 35 mm. (R) January 8, 1945. 64 mins. *With* Robert "Buzzy" Henry, Ralph Lewis. *Associate Producer* Martin Mooney *Director* Terry Morse *Screenplay* Raymond L. Schrock *Music Director* Walter Greene *Film Editor* George McGuire. Based on an original story by Taylor Caven.
© Pathe Industries, Inc., 19 June 1946; LP395.

The Dawn Express (Nazi Spy-Ring). © 1942. 7 reels, sd. (R) March 27, 1942. 66 mins. Presented by Producers Releasing Corp. An M&A Production. *With* Michael Whalen, Anne Nagel. *Producers* George M. Merrick, Max Alexander *Director* Albert Herman *Original Story and Screenplay* Arthur St. Claire *Music Director* Lee Zahler *Photographer* Eddie Linden *Film Editor* L.R. Brown.
© Producers Releasing Corp., 20 February 1942; LP11141.

Dead Men Walk. © 1943. 7 reels, sd. (R) February 10, 1943. 63 mins. *With* George Zucco, Mary Carlisle, Dwight Frye, Nedrick Young, Fern Emmett, Robert Strange, Hal Price, Sam Flint. *Producer* Sigmund Neufeld *Director* Sam

Newfield *Original Screenplay* Fred Myton *Music* Leo Erdody *Film Editor* Holbrook N. Todd *Cameraman* Jack Greenhalgh.
© Producers Releasing Corp., 26 January 1943; LP11811.

Dead or Alive. © 1944. 6 reels, sd. (R) November 9, 1944. 56 mins. ("Texas Rangers" series). *With* Tex Ritter, Dave O'Brien, Marjorie Clements, Guy Wilkerson, Charles King, Rebel Randall, Ray Bennett, Bud Osborne, Henry Hall, Ted Mapes, Reed Howes. *Producer* Arthur Alexander *Director* Elmer Clifton *Original Screenplay* Harry Fraser *Photographer* Robert Cline *Film Editor* Hugh Winn.
© PRC Pictures, Inc., 9 November 1944; LP13572.

Death Rides the Plains. See The Lone Rider in "Death Rides the Plains."

Delinquent Daughters. © 1944. 8 reels, sd. (R) July 15, 1944. 72 mins. PRC Pictures, Inc., for American Productions, Inc. *With* June Carlson, Fifi D'Orsay. *Producers* Donald C. McKean, Albert Herman *Director* Albert Herman *Original Screenplay* Arthur St. Claire *Music Director* Lee Zahler *Film Editor* George Merrick.
© PRC Pictures, Inc., 10 August 1944; LP13568.

Desperate Cargo. © 1941. 7 reels, sd. (R) July 4, 1941. 69 mins. *With* Ralph Byrd, Carol Hughes. *Producer* John T. Coyle *Director* William Beaudine *Screenplay* Morgan Cox, John T. Coyle *Photography* Jack Greenhalgh. Based on the story "Loot Below" by Eustace L. Adams.
© Producers Releasing Corp., 8 July 1941; LP10579.

Detour. © 1945. 7 reels, sd. (R) November 30, 1945. 69 mins. *With* Ann Savage, Tom Neal, Claudia Drake, Edmund MacDonald, Tim Ryan, Esther Howard, Roger Clark, Pat Gleason, Donald Brodie. *Associate Producer* Martin Mooney *Music* Leo Erdody *Art Director* Edward C. Jewel *Cameraman* Benjamin H. Kline *Editor* George McGuire *Director* Edgar G. Ulmer *Original Story and Screenplay* Martin Goldsmith. Adapted from the novel *Detour* by Tony Quinn.
© PRC Pictures, Inc., 7 November 1945; LP13599.

The Devil Bat. © 1940. 7 reels, sd. (R) December 13, 1940. 68 mins. *With* Bela Lugosi. *Producer* Jack Gallagher *Director* Jean Yarbrough *Original Story* George Bricker *Screenplay* John Thomas Neville *Photography* Arthur Martinelli *Film Editor* Holbrook N. Todd.
© Producers Releasing Corp., 17 December 1940; LP10133.

Devil Bat's Daughter. © 1946. 7 reels. (R) April 15, 1946. *With* Rosemary La Planche, John James. *Director* Frank Wisbar *Original Story* Leo J. McCarthy, Ernst Jaeger *Screenplay* Griffin Jay. *Appl. Author* PRC Pictures, Inc.
© Pathe Industries, Inc., 19 June 1946; LP396.

The Devil on Wheels. © 1947. 7 reels, sd., b&w, 35 mm. (R) March 2, 1947. 67 mins. *With* Jan Ford, Damian O'Flynn, Lenita Lane, Noreen Nash, Darryl Hickman. *Producer* Ben Stoloff *Director* Crane Wilbur *Original Story and*

A typically hard-boiled nightclub scene from "Delinquent Daughters," featuring June Carlson (right).

Screenplay Crane Wilbur *Music* Emil Cadkin *Musical Director* Irving Friedman *Film Editor* Alexander Troffey. From an original idea by Tony Sargent.
© Pathe Industries, Inc., 15 February 1947; LP844.

The Devil Riders. © 1943. 6 reels, sd. (R) November 5, 1943. 58 mins. ("Billy Carson" series). *With* Buster Crabbe, Al St. John, Patty McCarthy, Kermit Maynard, Charles Merton, Frank La Rue, Jack Ingram, George Chesebro, Ed Cassidy, Al Ferguson, Frank Ellis, Bert Dillard, Bud Osborne, Artie Ortego, Herman Hack, Roy Bucko, Buck Bucko. *Producer* Sigmund Neufeld *Director* Sam Newfield *Original Story and Screenplay* Joe O'Donnell *Film Editor* Bob Crandall.
© PRC Pictures, Inc., 6 November 1943; LP12358.

Dixie Jamboree. © 1945. 8 reels, sd. (R) August 15, 1944. 72 mins. *With* Frances Langford, Guy Kibbee. *Producer* Jack Schwarz *Director* Christy Cabanne *Screenplay* Sam Neuman *Music Arranger* Rudy Schrager *Film Editor* Robert Crandall. Based on original story by Lawrence E. Taylor.
© PRC Pictures, Inc., 15 August 1945; LP13618.

Don Ricardo Returns. © 1946. 7 reels, sd., 35 mm. (R) November 5, 1946. 63 mins. Presented by PRC Pictures, Inc. *With* Fred Colby, Isabelita. *Producer* J.S. Burkett *Director* T.O. Morse *Original Story* Johnston McCully *Screenplay*

Jack DeWitt, Renault Duncan *Music* Alexander Steinert *Film Editor* George McGuire.
© Pathe Industries, Inc., 5 November 1946; LP686.

Double Cross. © 1941. 7 reels, sd. (R) June 27, 1941. 61 mins. *With* Kane Richmond, Pauline Moore. *Producer* John G. Bachmann *Director* Albert Kelley *Original Story* John A. Albert *Screenplay* Milton Raison, Ron Ferguson *Photography* Arthur Martinelli.
© Producers Releasing Corp., 27 June 1941; LP10578.

Down Missouri Way. © 1946. 8 reels, sd., 35 mm. (R) August 15, 1946. 75 mins. *With* Martha O'Driscoll, William Wright. *Director* Joseph Berne *Original Screenplay* Sam Neuman. *Appl. Author* PRC Pictures, Inc.
© Pathe Industries, Inc., 1 August 1946; LP455.

The Drifter. © 1943. 6 reels, sd. (R) December 20, 1943. 60 mins. ("Billy Carson" series.) *With* Buster Crabbe, Al St. John, Carol Parker, Kermit Maynard, Jack Ingram, Roy Brent, George Chesebro, Ray Bennett, Jimmy Aubrey, Slim Whitaker, Wally West. *Producer* Sigmund Neufeld *Director* Sam Newfield *Original Story and Screenplay* Patricia Harper *Film Editor* Holbrook Todd.
© PRC Pictures, Inc., 1 December 1943; LP12385.

Driftin' River. © 1946. 6 reels, sd., 35 mm. (R) October 7, 1946. 59 mins. Presented by PRC Pictures, Inc. *With* Eddie Dean, Shirley Patterson. *Director* Robert Emmett Tansey *Original Screenplay* Frances Kavanaugh *Music Director* Karl Hajos *Music Arranger* Walter Greene *Film Editor* Hugh Winn.
© Pathe Industries, Inc., 1 October 1946; LP625.

Duke of the Navy. © 1942. 7 reels, sd. (R) January 23, 1942. 65 mins. *With* Ralph Byrd, Veda Ann Borg. *Producer* John T. Coyle *Director* William Beaudine *Story and Screenplay* Gerald D. Adams, William Beaudine, John T. Coyle *Music Director* Clarence Wheeler *Film Editor* Guy V. Thayer, Jr.
© Producers Releasing Corp., 5 January 1942; LP11130.

Emergency Landing. © 1941. 7 reels, sd. (R) May 9, 1941. 79 mins. *With* Carol Hughes, Forrest Tucker. *Producer* Jed Buell *Director* William Beaudine *Original Story and Screenplay* Martin Mooney *Photography* Jack Greenhalgh *Film Editor* Robert Crandall.
© Producers Releasing Corp., 23 May 1941; LP10532.

The Enchanted Forest. © 1945. 9 reels, sd., color. (R) December 8, 1945. 78 mins. *With* Edmund Lowe, Brenda Joyce. *Director* Lew Landers *Original Story* John Lebar *Screenplay* Robert Lee Johnson, John Lebar, Lou Brock *Adaptation* Sam Neuman, Lou Brock *Music* Albert Hay Malotte.
© PRC Pictures, Inc., 17 November 1945; LP13641.

Enemy of the Law. © 1945. 6 reels, sd. (R) May 7, 1945. 59 mins. ("Texas Rangers" series.) *With* Tex Ritter, Dave O'Brien, Guy Wilkerson, Kay Hughes, Jack Ingram, Charles King, Frank Ellis, Kermit Maynard, Henry Hall, Karl Hackett, Edward Cassidy, Ben Corbett. *Producer* Arthur Alexander *Direction*

and Original Screenplay Harry Fraser *Music Director* Lee Zahler *Photographer* Jack Greenhalgh *Film Editor* Holbrook N. Todd.
© PRC Pictures, Inc., 7 May 1945; LP13650.

Federal Fugitives. © 1941. 7 reels, sd. (R) March 29, 1941. 66 mins. *With* Neil Hamilton. *Producer* John T. Coyle *Director* William Beaudine *Original Story and Screenplay* Martin Mooney *Music Director* Alberto Colombo *Editor* Guy V. Thayer, Jr.
© Producers Releasing Corp., 20 March 1941; LP10390.

Fighting Bill Carson. © 1945. 6 reels, sd. (R) October 31, 1945. 51 mins. ("Billy Carson" series.) *With* Buster Crabbe, Al St. John, Kay Hughes, I. Stanford Jolley, Kermit Maynard, John L. "Bob" Cason, Budd Buster, Bud Osborne, Charles King. *Producer* Sigmund Neufeld *Director* Sam Newfield *Original Story and Screenplay* Louise Rousseau *Music Director* Frank Sanucci *Film Editor* Holbrook N. Todd.
© PRC Pictures, Inc., 31 October 1945; LP13658.

Fighting Valley. © 1943. 6 reels, sd. (R) August 1, 1943. 59 mins. ("Texas Rangers" series.) *With* Dave O'Brien, Jim Newill, Guy Wilkerson, Patti McCarthy, John Merton, Robert Rice, Stanley Price, Mary MacLaren, John Elliott, Charles King, Dan White, Carl Mathews, Curley Dresden, Jimmy Aubrey, Jess Cavin. *Producers* Alfred Stern, Arthur Alexander *Direction and Original Screenplay* Oliver Drake *Music Director* Lee Zahler *Photographer* Ira Morgan *Film Editor* Charles Henkel, Jr.
© Producers Releasing Corp., 8 August 1943; LP12170.

Flaming Bullets. © 1945. 6 reels, sd. (R) October 15, 1945. 59 mins. ("Texas Rangers" series.) *With* Tex Ritter, Dave O'Brien, Guy Wilkerson, Patricia Knox, Charles King, Bud Osborne, I. Stanford Jolley, Bob Duncan, Kermit Maynard, Dick Alexander, Dan White. *Producer* Arthur Alexander *Direction and Original Screenplay* Harry Fraser *Music Director* Lee Zahler.
© PRC Pictures, Inc., 15 October 1945; LP13573.

The Flying Serpent. © 1946. 6 reels, sd. (R) February 20, 1946. 59 mins. *With* George Zucco. *Producer* Sigmund Neufeld *Director* Sherman Scott *Original Story and Screenplay* John T. Neville *Music Director* Leo Erdody *Film Editor* Holbrook N. Todd.
© PRC Pictures, Inc., 1 February 1946; LP84.

Fog Island. © 1945. 7 reels, sd. (R) February 15, 1945. 72 mins. *With* Lionel Atwill, George Zucco, Veda Ann Borg, Jerome Cowan. *Producer* Leon Fromkess *Director* Terry Morse *Screenplay* Pierre Gendron *Film Editor* George McGuire. Based on the play *Angel Island* by Bernadine Angus.
© PRC Pictures, Inc., 15 February 1945; LP13610.

Frontier Crusader. (R) June 1, 1940. 62 mins. *With* Tim McCoy, Dorothy Short, Lou Fulton, Karl Hackett, Ted Adams, John Merton, Forrest Taylor, Hal Price, Frank La Rue, Kenne Duncan, George Chesebro, Frank Ellis, Carl Mathews, Reed Howes, Herman Hack, Sherry Tansey, Lane Bradford, Ray Henderson. *Producer* Sigmund Neufeld *Director* Peter Stewart (Sam Newfield)

Someone wants to be sure that Neil Hamilton (right) gets the point in "Federal Fugitives."

Story Arthur Durlam *Screenplay* Wiliam Lively *Music Director* Lou Porter *Photography* Jack Greenhalgh *Film Editor* Holbrook N. Todd.

Frontier Fugitives. © 1945. 6 reels, sd. (R) September 1, 1945. 58 mins. ("Texas Rangers" series.) *With* Dave O'Brien, Tex Ritter, Lorraine Miller, Guy Wilkerson, I. Stanford Jolley, Jack Ingram, Frank Ellis, Jack Hendricks, Charles King, Karl Hackett, Budd Buster. *Producer* Arthur Alexander *Director* Harry Fraser *Original Screenplay* Elmer Clifton *Music Director* Lee Zahler *Photographer* Robert Cline *Film Editor* Holbrook N. Todd.
© PRC Pictures, Inc., 1 September 1945; LP13640.

Frontier Outlaws. © 1944. 6 reels, sd. (R) March 4, 1944. 58 mins. ("Billy Carson" series.) *With* Buster Crabbe, Al St. John, Frances Gladwin, Marin Sais, Charles King, Jack Ingram, Kermit Maynard, Edward Cassidy, Emmett Lynn, Budd Buster, Frank Ellis. *Producer* Sigmund Neufeld *Director* Sam Newfield *Original Story and Screenplay* Joe O'Donnell *Film Editor* Holbrook N. Todd.
© PRC Pictures, Inc., 4 April 1944; LP13606.

Fugitive of the Plains. See **Billy the Kid** in "Fugitive of the Plains."

Fuzzy Settles Down. © 1944. 6 reels, sd., 35mm. (R) July 25, 1944. 60 mins. ("Billy Carson" series.) *With* Buster Crabbe, Al St. John, Patti McCarthy, Charles King, John Merton, Frank McCarroll, Hal Price, John Elliott, Edward Cassidy, Robert Hill, Ted Mapes, Tex Palmer. *Producer* Sigmund Neufeld *Direc-*

tor Sam Newfield *Original Story and Screenplay* Louise Rousseau *Film Editor* Holbrook N. Todd.
© PRC Pictures, Inc., 12 July 1944; LP493.

Gallant Lady. © 1942. 7 reels, sd. (R) May 29, 1942. 63 mins. *With* Rose Hobart, Sidney Blackmer. *Producer* Lester Cutler *Director* William Beaudine *Screenplay* Arthur St. Claire *Music Director* Lee Zahler *Film Editor* Fred Bain. From original story by Octavus Roy Cohen.
© Producers Releasing Corp., 23, May 1942; LP11320.

Gambling Daughters. © 1941. 7 reels, sd. (R) August 1, 1941. 67 mins. *With* Cecilia Parker, Roger Pryor. *Producer* T.H. Richmond *Director* Max Nosseck *Original Story* Sidney Sheldon, Ben Roberts *Screenplay* Joel Kay, Arnold Phillips.
© Producers Releasing Corp., 26 July 1941; LP10654.

Gangster's Den. © 1945. 6 reels, sd. (R) June 14, 1945. 55 mins. ("Billy Carson" series.) *With* Buster Crabbe, Al St. John, Sidney Logan, Charles King, Emmett Lynn, Kermit Maynard, Edward Cassidy, I. Stanford Jolley, George Chesebro, Karl Hackett, Michael Owen, Bob Cason, Wally West. *Producer* Sigmund Neufeld *Director* Sam Newfield *Original Story and Screenplay* George Plympton *Film Editor* Holbrook N. Todd.
© PRC Pictures, Inc., 14 July 1945; LP13607.

Gangsters of the Frontier. © 1944. 6 reels, sd. (R) September 21, 1944. 56 mins. ("Texas Rangers" series.) *With* Tex Ritter, Dave O'Brien, Guy Wilkerson, Patti McCarthy, Betty Miles, Harry Harvey, I. Stanford Jolley, Charles King, Marshall Reed, Clarke Stevens. *Producer* Arthur Alexander *Direction and Original Screenplay* Elmer Clifton *Music Director* Lee Zahler *Photographer* Robert Cline *Film Editor* Charles Henkel, Jr.
© PRC Pictures, Inc., 25 September 1944; LP13561.

Gashouse Kids. © 1946. 7 reels, sd., 35 mm. (R) October 28, 1946. 68 mins. *With* Robert Lowery. *Producer* Sigmund Neufeld *Director* Sam Newfield *Original Story* Elsie and George Bricker *Screenplay* Elsie and George Bricker, Raymond L. Schrock *Music Director* Leo Erdody *Film Editor* Holbrook N. Todd.
© PRC Pictures, Inc., 7 October 1946; LP685.

Gas House Kids Go West. © 1947. sd., 35 mm. b&w. (R) June 12, 1947. 62 mins. *With* Carl "Alfalfa" Switzer, Bennie Bartlett, Rudy Wissler, Tommy Bond, Emory Parnell, Chili Williams, Vince Barnett, William Wright, Lela Bliss, Ronn Marvin, Ray Dolciame. A Ben Stoloff Production. *Producer* Sam Baerwitz *Director* William Beaudine *Original Story* Sam Baerwitz *Screenplay* Robert E. Kent, Robert A. McGowan, Eugene Conrad *Music* Hans Sommer *Film Editor* Harry Reynolds.
© Pathe Industries, Inc., 28 June 1947; LP1139.

The Gas House Kids In Hollywood. © 1947. sd., b&w, 35 mm. (R) August 23, 1947. 63 mins. A Ben Stoloff production. (Eagle-Lion Films, Inc.) *With* Carl "Alfalfa" Switzer, Rudy Wissler, Benny Bartlett, Tommy Bond, James Burke.

The mystery is neatly wrapped up in this climactic scene from "Gas House Kids in Hollywood," with Carl "Alfalfa" Switzer (extreme right) and Tommy Bond (kneeling, left of Switzer).

Producer Sam Baerwitz *Director* Edward Cahn *Original Screenplay* Robert E. Kent *Music* Albert Glasser *Film Editor* W. Donn Hayes.
© Pathe Industries, Inc., 8 September 1947; LP1185.

Gentlemen with Guns. © 1946. 6 reels, sd. (R) March 27, 1946. 52 mins. ("Billy Carson" series.) *With* Buster Crabbe, Al St. John, Patricia Knox, Steve Darrell, George Chesebro, Karl Hackett, Budd Buster, Frank Ellis, George Morrell. *Producer* Sigmund Neufeld *Director* Sam Newfield *Original Story and Screenplay* Fred Myton *Music Director* Lee Zahler. *Appl. Author* PRC Pictures, Inc.
© Pathe Industries, Inc., 22 June 1946; LP414.

The Ghost and the Guest. © 1943. 6 reels, sd. (R) April 19, 1943. 61 mins. *With* James Dunn, Florence Rice, Mabel Todd, Sam McDaniel, Robert Dudley, Eddy Chandler, Jim Toney, Robert Bice, Renee Carson, Tony Ward, Anthony Caruso, Eddie Foster. *Producers* Arthur Alexander, Alfred Stern *Director* William Nigh *Original Story* Milt Gross *Screenplay* Morey Amsterdam *Music*

Director Lee Zahler *Photographer* Robert Cline *Film Editor* Charles Henkel, Jr. *Art Director* James Altweid.
© PRC Pictures, Inc., 19 April 1943; LP13619.

Ghost of Hidden Valley. © 1946. 6 reels, sd. (R) June 3, 1946. 56 mins. ("Billy Carson" series.) *With* Buster Crabbe, Al St. John, Jean Carlin, John Meredith, Charles King, Karl Hackett, Jimmy Aubrey, John L. "Bob" Cason, Silver Harr, Zon Murray, George Morrell, Bert Dillard, Cecil Trenton. *Producer* Sigmund Neufeld *Director* Sam Newfield *Original Story and Screenplay* Ellen Coyle *Music Director* Lee Zahler. *Appl. Author* PRC Pictures, Inc.
© Pathe Industries, Inc., 3 June 1946; LP417.

Ghost Town Renegades. © 1947. sd., 35 mm. b&w. (R) July 26, 1947. 57 mins. *With* "Lash" La Rue, Al St. John, Jennifer Holt, Lee Roberts, Jack Ingram, Terry Frost, Steve Clark, Lane Bradford, Henry Hall, William Fawcett, Mason Wynn, Dee Cooper. *Producer* Jerry Thomas *Director* Ray Taylor *Screenplay* Patricia Harper *Music* Walter Greene *Film Editor* Joe Gluck.
© Pathe Industries, Inc., 17 June 1947; LP1134.

The Girl from Monterey. © 1943. 6 reels, sd. (R) October 4, 1943. 58 mins. *With* Armida, Edgar Kennedy, Veda Ann Borg, Jack La Rue, Terry Frost, Anthony Caruso, Charles Williams, Bryant Washburn, Guy Zannett, Wheeler Oakman. *Producer* Jack Schwarz *Associate Producer* Harry D. Edwards *Director* Wallace Fox *Authors* George Green, Robert Gordon *Screenplay* Arthur Hoerl *Art Director* Frank Sylos *Musical Director* Mahlon Merrick *Musical Supervisor* David Chudnow *Cameraman* Marcel LePicard *Film Editor* Robert Crandall.
© PRC Pictures, Inc., 19 October 1943; LP12330.

Girls in Chains. © 1943. 7 reels, sd. (R) May 17, 1943. 71 mins. Presented by Producers Releasing Corp. Atlantis Pictures Corp. *With* Arline Judge, Roger Clark, Robin Raymond, Barbara Pepper, Dorothy Burgess, Clancy Cooper, Allan Byron, Patricia Knox, Sidney Melton, Russell Gaige, Emmett Lynn, Richard Clarke, Betty Blythe, Peggy Stewart, Beverly Boyd, Bob Hill, Henry Hall, Mrs. Gardener Crane, Crane Whitley, Francis Ford. *Producer* Peter R. van Duinen *Director* Edgar G. Ulmer *Screenplay* Albert Beich *Music Score* Leo Erdody *Editor* Charles Henkel, Jr. *Cameraman* Ira Morgan. Based on a story by Edgar G. Ulmer.
© Producers Releasing Corp., 17 April 1943; LP11980.

Girls' Town. © 1942. 7 reels, sd. (R) March 6, 1942. 68 mins. A Preference picture. *With* June Storey, Edith Fellows. *Producers* Lou Brock, Jack Schwarz *Director* Victor Halperin *Screenplay* Gene Kerr, Victor McLeod *Music Director* Lee Zahler *Film Editor* Martin G. Cohn.
© Producers Releasing Corp., 25 January 1942; LP11136.

Goose Step. See Beasts of Berlin.

The Great Mike. © 1944. 8 reels, sd. (R) November 15, 1944. 73 mins. *With* Robert Henry, Stuart Erwin. *Producer* Leon Fromkess *Director* Wallace W. Fox

Original Story Martin Mooney *Screenplay* Raymond L. Schrock *Music Score* Lee Zahler *Film Editor* Hugh Winn.
© PRC Pictures, Inc., 15 November 1944; LP13638.

Gun Code. © 1940. 6 reels, sd. (R) July 29, 1940. 57 mins. *With* Tim McCoy, Inna Gest (Ina Guest), Lou Fulton, Alden Chase, Ted Adams, Dave O'Brien, Carleton Young, Robert Winkler, John Elliott, George Chesebro, Jack Richardson, Carl Mathews. *Producer* Sigmund Neufeld *Director* Peter Stewart (Sam Newfield) *Original Screenplay* Joseph O'Donnell *Music Director* Lou Porter *Photography* Jack Greenhalgh *Film Editor* Holbrook N. Todd.
© Producers Releasing Corp., 25 July 1940; LP9835.

Guns of the Law. © 1944. 6 reels, sd. (R) April 10, 1944. 55 mins. ("Texas Rangers" series.) *With* Dave O'Brien, Jim Newill, Guy Wilkerson, Budd Buster, Charles King, Jack Ingram, Robert Kortman, Robert Barron, Frank McCarroll, Bud Osborne. *Producer* Arthur Alexander *Direction and Screenplay* Elmer Clifton *Music Director* Lee Zahler.
© PRC Pictures, Inc., 31 March 1944; LP437.

Gunsmoke Mesa. © 1944. 6 reels, sd. (R) January 3, 1944. 59 mins. ("Texas Rangers" series.) *With* Dave O'Brien, Jim Newill, Patti McCarty, Guy Wilkerson, Jack Ingram, Kermit Maynard, Robert Barron, Dick Alexander, Michael Vallon, Roy Brent, Jack Rockwell. *Producer* Arthur Alexander *Director* Harry Fraser *Original Screenplay* Elmer Clifton *Music Director* Lee Zahler *Photographer* Ira Morgan *Film Editor* Charles Henkel, Jr.
© PRC Pictures, Inc., 1 January 1944; LP12414.

Hard Guy. © 1941. 7 reels, sd. (R) October 17, 1941. 68 mins. *With* Jack La Rue, Mary Healy. *Producer* George M. Merrick *Director* Elmer Clifton *Original Story and Screenplay* Oliver Drake *Photographer* Eddie Linden *Film Editor* Charles Henkel.
© Producers Releasing Corp., 26 September 1941; LP10724.

Harvest Melody. © 1943. 7 reels, sd. (R) November 22, 1943. 71 mins. *With* Rosemary Lane, Johnny Downs, Sheldon Leonard, Charlotte Synters, Luis Alberni, Claire Rochelle, Syd Saylor, Marjorie Manners, Sunny Fox, Henry Hall, Billy Nelson, Frances Gladwin, The Radio Rogues, The Vigilantes, Eddie LeBaron Orchestra. *Producer* Walter Colmes *Director* Sam Newfield *Screenplay* Allan Gale *Authors* Martin Mooney, Andre Lamb *Art Director* Frank Sylos *Musical Supervisor* David Chudnow *Music Director* Jay Cherniss *Songs* Harry Akst, Leo Shuken, Walter Colmes, Benny Davis *Cameraman* James Brown *Film Editor* Holbrook N. Todd.
© PRC Pictures, Inc., 22 November 1943; LP13569.

Heartaches. © 1947. sd., b&w, 71 mins. PRC Pictures, Inc. A Ben Stoloff Production. *With* Sheila Ryan, Edward Norris. *Producer* Marvin D. Stahl *Director* Basil Wrangell *Original Story* Monty F. Collins, Julian I. Peyser *Screenplay* George Bricker *Incidental Music* Emil Cadkin *Music Director* Irving Friedman *Film Editor* Charles Gross, Jr.
© Pathe Industries, Inc., 27 May 1947; LP1136.

Top: Jack La Rue (left) has some explaining to do to Kane Richmond in this scene from "Hard Guy." Bottom: Margaret Lindsay (right) in "Her Sister's Secret."

Hell's Devils. See Beasts of Berlin and Goose Step.

Her Sister's Secret. © 1946. 9 reels, sd., 35mm. (R) September 23, 1946. 85 mins. Presented by PRC Pictures, Inc. *With* Nancy Coleman, Margaret Lindsay, Philip Reed. *Producer* Henry Brash *Director* Edgar G. Ulmer *Screenplay* Anne Green *Music* Hans Sommer *Film Editor* Jack W. Ogilvie *Cameraman* Franz Planer. Based on the novel *Dark Angel* by Gina Kaus.
© Pathe Industries, Inc., 12 September 1946; LP598.

His Brother's Ghost. © 1945. 6 reels, sd. (R) February 3, 1945. 54 mins. ("Billy Carson" series.) *With* Buster Crabbe, Al St. John, Charles King, Karl Hackett, Archie Hall, Roy Brent, Bud Osborne, Bob Cason, Frank McCarroll, George Morrell. *Producer* Sigmund Neufeld *Director* Sam Newfield *Original Story and Screenplay* George Milton *Film Editor* Holbrook N. Todd.
© PRC Pictures, Inc., 3 March 1945; LP13651.

Hold That Woman! © 1940. 7 reels, sd. (R) July 15, 1940. 67 mins. *With* James Dunn, Frances Gifford. *Producer* Sigmund Neufeld *Director* Sherman Scott (Sam Newfield) *Original Story* Raymond L. Schrock, William Pierce *Screenplay* George Bricker *Music Director* David Chudnow *Cameraman* Jack Greenhalgh *Film Editor* Holbrook N. Todd.
© Producers Releasing Corp., 22 June 1940; LP9820.

Hollywood and Vine. © 1945. 6 reels, sd. (R) April 25, 1945. 58 mins. *With* James Ellison, Wanda McKay. *Producer* Leon Fromkess *Director* Alexis Thurn-Taxis *Original Story* Edith Watkins, Charles Williams, Robert Wilmot *Screenplay* Edith Watkins, Charles Williams.
© PRC Pictures, Inc., 25 April 1945; LP13579.

House of Errors. © 1942. 7 reels, sd. (R) April 10, 1942. 65 mins. A Beaumont production. *With* Harry Langdon. *Director* Bernard B. Ray *Original Story* Harry Langdon *Screenplay* Ewart Adamson, Eddie M. Davis *Music Director* Lee Zahler *Film Editor* Dan Milner.
© Producers Releasing Corp., 20 February 1942; LP11183.

How Doooo You Do? © 1946. 8 reels, sd. (R) December 24, 1945. 80 mins. *With* Bert Gordon, Harry Von Zell. *Director* Ralph Murphy *Original Story* Harry Sauber *Screenplay* Harry Sauber, Joseph Carole.
© PRC Pictures, Inc., 7 January 1946; LP15.

I Accuse My Parents. © 1944. 7 reels, sd. (R) November 4, 1944. 70 mins. An Alexander-Stern production. *With* Robert Lowell, Mary Beth Hughes. *Producer* Max Alexander *Director* Sam Newfield *Original Story* Arthur Caesar *Screenplay* Harry Fraser, Marjorie Dudley *Music Director* Lee Zahler *Film Editor* Charles Henkel, Jr.
© PRC Pictures, Inc., 15 December 1944; LP13011.

I Ring Doorbells. © 1946. 7 reels, sd. (R) February 25, 1945. 64 mins. *With* Robert Shayne, Ann Gwynne. *Director* Frank Strayer *Screenplay* Dick Irving Hyland *Adaptation* Dick Irving Hyland, Raymond L. Schrock. Based on the book by Russel Birdwell.
© PRC Pictures, Inc., 12 January 1946; LP26.

Wallace Ford (center) breaks it up in "Inside the Law."

I Take This Oath. © 1940. 7 reels, sd. (R) May 20, 1940. 67 mins. Presented by Sig Neufeld. *With* Gordon Jones. *Director* Sherman Scott (Sam Newfield) *Original Story* William A. Ullman, Jr. *Screenplay* George Bricker *Music Director*, David Chudnow *Cameraman* Jack Greenhalgh *Film Editor* Holbrook Todd.
 © Producers Releasing Corp., 14 May 1940; LP9805.

I'm from Arkansas. © 1944. 7 reels, sd. (R) October 31, 1944. 70 mins. *With* Slim Summerville, El Brendel. *Producers* E.H. Kleinert, Irving Vershel *Director* Lew Landers *Original Story* Marcy Klauber *Screenplay* Marcy Klauber, Joseph Carole *Music Director* Eddie Paul *Film Editor* John Link.
 © PRC Pictures, Inc., 15 December 1944; LP13010.

Inside the Law. © 1942. 7 reels, sd. (R) May 8, 1942. 62 mins. *With* Wallace Ford. *Producer* Dixon R. Harwin *Director* Hamilton MacFadden *Original Screenplay* Jack Natteford *Music Director* David Chudnow *Film Editor* Carl Pierson.
 © Producers Releasing Corp., 27 April 1942; LP11285.

The Invisible Killer. (R) November 14, 1939. *With* Grace Bradley, Roland Drew. *Director* Sam Newfield (Sherman Scott).

Isle of Forgotten Sins. © 1943. 8 reels, sd. (R) August 15, 1943. 82 mins. Atlantis Pictures Corp. Presented by PRC. *With* John Carradine, Gale Sondergaard, Sidney Toler, Frank Fenton, Veda Ann Borg, Rita Quigley, Rick Vallin, Betty Amann, Tala Birell, Patti McCarty, Marian Colby, William Edmonds. *Producer* Peter R. Van Duinen *Director* Edgar G. Ulmer *Author* Raymond L. Schrock *Screenplay* Raymond L. Schrock *Art Director* Fred Preble

Music Leo Erdody *Cameraman* Ira Morgan *Film Editor* Charles Henkel, Jr. Based on an original story by Edgar G. Ulmer.
© Producers Releasing Corp., 10 July 1943; LP12133.

It's a Joke, Son! © 1947. sd., b&w, 35 mm. (R) January 15, 1947. 64 mins. (Eagle-Lion Films, Inc.) *With* Kenny Delmar, Una Merkel. *Director* Ben Stoloff *Original Screenplay* Robert Kent, Paul Gerard Smith.
© Pathe Industries, Inc., 8 February 1947; LP818.

Jive Junction. © 1943. 8 reels, sd. (R) December 16, 1943. 67 mins. *With* Tina Thayer, Dickie Moore, Gerra Young, Johnny Michaels, Jack Wagner, Jan Wiley, Beverly Boyd, Bill Halligan, Johnny Duncan, Johnny Clark, Frederick Feher, Coral Ashley, Odessa Laurin, Bob McKenzie. *Producer* Leon Fromkess *Director* Edgar G. Ulmer *Authors* Malvin Wald, Walter Doniger *Screenplay* Irving Wallace, Walter Doniger, Malvin Wald *Art Director* Frank Sylso *Dance Director* Don Gallaher *Cameraman* Ira Morgan *Film Editor* Robert Crandall.
© PRC Pictures, Inc., 20 December 1943; LP13585.

Jungle Man. © 1941. 6 reels, sd. (R) October 10, 1941. 63 mins. *With* Buster Crabbe. *Producer* T.H. Richmond *Director* Harry Fraser *Original Story and Screenplay* Rita Douglas *Photography* Mervyn Freeman *Film Editor* Holbrook N. Todd.
© Producers Releasing Corp., 27 September 1941; LP10897.

Jungle Siren. © 1942. 7 reels, sd. (R) August 21, 1942. 68 mins. *With* Ann Corio, Buster Crabbe. *Producer* Sigmund Neufeld *Director* Sam Newfield *Original Story* George W. Sayre, Milton Raison *Screenplay* George W. Sayre, Sam Robins *Film Editor* Holbrook N. Todd.
© Producers Releasing Corp., 7 August 1942; LP11504.

The Kid Sister. © 1945. 6 reels, sd. (R) February 6, 1945. 56 mins. *With* Judy Clark, Roger Pryor. *Producer* Sigmund Neufeld *Director* Sam Newfield *Original Story and Screenplay* Fred Myton *Music Director* David Chudnow *Film Editor* Holbrook N. Todd.
© PRC Pictures, Inc., 6 February 1945; LP13639.

The Kid Rides Again. See Billy the Kid in "The Kid Rides Again."

Killer at Large. © 1947. sd., b&w, 35 mm. (R) May 31, 1947. 63 mins. (Eagle-Lion) *With* Robert Lowery, Anabel Shaw. *Producer* Buck Gottlieb *Director* William Beaudine *Original Screenplay* Fenton Earnshaw, Tom Blackburn *Music* Albert Glasser *Film Editor* Harry Reynolds.
© Pathe Industries, Inc., 31 May 1947; LP1047.

Lady Chaser. © 1946. 6 reels, sd. 35mm. PRC Pictures, Inc. *Producer* Sigmund Neufeld *Director* Sam Newfield *Original Story* G.T. Fleming-Roberts *Screenplay* Fred Myton *Film Editor* Holbrook N. Todd.
© Pathe Industries, Inc., 25 November 1946; LP715.

The Lady Confesses. © 1945. 7 reels, sd. (R) May 16, 1945. 64 mins. *With* Mary Beth Hughes, Hugh Beaumont. *Producer* Alfred Stern *Director* Sam

Newfield *Original Story* Irwin R. Franklyn *Screenplay* Helen Martin *Music Director* Lee Zahler *Film Editor* Holbrook N. Todd.
©PRC Pictures, Inc., 16 May 1945; LP13595.

Lady from Chungking. © 1943. 7 reels, sd. (R) December 21, 1942. 70 mins. *With* Anna May Wong, Harold Huber. *Producers* Alfred Stern, Arthur Alexander *Director* William Nigh *Original Story* Milton Raison, Sam Robins *Screenplay* Sam Robins *Music Director* Lee Zahler *Photographer* Marcel LePicard *Film Editor* Charles Henkel, Jr.
© Producers Releasing Corp., 5 February 1943; LP11835.

Lady in the Death House. © 1944. 6 reels, sd. (R) March 15, 1944. 64 mins. *With* Lionel Atwill, Jean Parker. *Producer* Jack Schwarz *Director* Steve Sekely *Original Story* Frederick C. Davis *Screenplay* Harry O. Hoyt *Original Music* Jan Gray *Music Supervision* David Chudnow *Film Editor* Robert O. Crandall.
© PRC Pictures, Inc., 15 March 1944; LP13583.

Larceny in Her Heart. © 1946. 7 reels, sd. 35mm. (R) July 10, 1946. 68 mins. Presented by PRC Pictures. *With* Hugh Beaumont, Cheryl Walker. *Producer* Sigmund Neufeld *Director* Sam Newfield *Screenplay* Raymond L. Schrock *Music Director* Leo Erdody. Based upon original characters and story by Brett Halliday. *Appl. Author* PRC Pictures, Inc.
© Pathe Industries, Inc., 18 June 1946; LP386.

Law and Order. See **Billy the Kid** in "**Law and Order.**"

Law of the Lash. © 1947. sd., b&w, 35 mm. (R) February 28, 1947. 53 mins. *With* "Lash" La Rue, Al St. John, Mary Scott, Lee Roberts, Jack O'Shea, John Elliott, Charles King, Carl Mathews, Matty Roubert, Slim Whitaker, Ted French, Dick Cramer, Brad Slaven. *Producer* Jerry Thomas *Director* Ray Taylor *Original Screenplay* William L. Nolte *Music* Albert Glasser *Film Editor* Hugh Winn.
© Pathe Industries, Inc., 6 February 1947; LP838.

Law of the Saddle. See **The Lone Rider** in "**Law of the Saddle.**"

Law of the Timber. © 1941. 7 reels, sd. 35 mm. (R) December 19, 1941. 68 mins. Presented by Producers Releasing Corp. *With* Marjorie Reynolds, Monte Blue. *Director* Bernard B. Ray *Screenplay* Jack Natteford *Music Director* Clarence E. Wheeler *Film Editor* Carl Himm. Adapted from "The Speck on the Wall" by James Oliver Curwood. *Appl. Author* PRC Pictures, Inc.
© Producers Releasing Corp., 7 December 1941 (in notice: 1942); LP523.

Lighthouse. © 1947. 6 reels, sd., b&w, 35 mm. (R) January 10, 1947. 62 mins. A Sunset production. *With* John Litel, June Lang, Don Castle. *Producer* Franklin Gilbert *Director* Frank Wisbar *Original Story and Adaptation* Don Martin *Screenplay* Robert Churchill *Music* Ernest Gold *Film Editor* Robert Jahns.
© Pathe Industries, Inc., 10 January 1947; LP792.

Lightning Raiders. © 1946. 6 reels, sd. (R) January 7, 1946. 61 mins. ("Billy Carson" series.) *With* Buster Crabbe, Al St. John, Mady Lawrence, Ray Brent,

Sally Eilers, Charles Arnt, and Warren William in a lobby card shot for "Out of the Night" ("Strange Illusion").

Henry Hall, Steve Darrell, Marin Sais, Al Ferguson, Karl Hackett, I. Stanford Jolley. *Producer* Sigmund Neufeld *Director* Sam Newfield *Original Story and Screenplay* Elmer Clifton *Music Director* Lee Zahler *Film Editor* Holbrook N. Todd.
© PRC Pictures, Inc., 22 June 1946; LP413.

The Lone Rider Ambushed. ©1941. 6 reels, sd. (R) August 29, 1941. 63 mins. ("Lone Rider" series.) *With* George Houston, Al St. John, Maxine Leslie, Frank Hagney, Jack Ingram, Hal Price, Ted Adams, George Chesebro, Ralph Peters, Steve Clark, Carl Mathews, Charles King. *Producer* Sigmund Neufeld *Director* Sam Newfield *Original Screenplay* Oliver Drake *Music* Johnny Lange, Lew Porter *Film Editor* Holbrook N. Todd.
© Producers Releasing Corp., 21 August 1941; LP10676.

The Lone Rider and the Bandit. © 1942. 6 reels, sd. (R) January 16, 1942. 54 mins. ("Lone Rider" series.) *With* George Houston, Al St. John, Dennis Moore, Vicki Lester, Glenn Strange, Jack Ingram, Milt Kibbee, Carl Sepulveda, Slim Andrews, Eddie Dean, Slim Whitaker, Hal Price, Kenne Duncan, Curley Dresden. *Producer* Sigmund Neufeld *Director* Sam Newfield *Screenplay* Steve Braxton *Photography* Jack Greenhalgh *Film Editor* Holbrook N. Todd.
© Producers Releasing Corp., 14 January 1942; LP11046.

The Lone Rider Crosses the Rio. © 1941. 6 reels, sd. (R) February 28, 1941. ("Lone Rider" series.) *With* George Houston, Al St. John, Roquell Verrin, Jay Wilsey (Buffalo Bill, Jr.), Charles King, Alden Chase, Julian Rivero, Thornton Edwards, Howard Masters, Frank Ellis, Philip Turich, Frank Hagney, Curley Dresden, Sherry Tansey, Steve Clark. *Producer* Sigmund Neufeld *Director* Sam Newfield *Original Screenplay* William Lively *Film Editor* Holbrook N. Todd.
© Producers Releasing Corp., 24 February 1941; LP10271.

The Lone Rider Fights Back. © 1941. 6 reels, sd. (R) November 7, 1941. 64 mins. ("Lone Rider" series.) *With* George Houston, Al St. John, Dorothy Short, Frank Hagney, Dennis Moore, Charles King, Frank Ellis, Hal Price, Jack O'Shea, Merrill McCormack. *Producer* Sigmund Neufeld *Director* Sam Newfield *Original Screenplay* Joseph O'Donnell *Music* Johnny Lange, Lew Porter *Film Editor* Holbrook N. Todd.
© Producers Releasing Corp., 16 October 1941; LP10784.

The Lone Rider in Cheyenne. © 1942. 6 reels, sd. (R) March 20, 1942. 59 mins. ("Lone Rider" series.) *With* George Houston, Al St. John, Dennis Moore, Ella Neal, Roy Barcroft, Kenne Duncan, Lynton Brent, Milt Kibbee, Jack Holmes, Karl Hackett, Jack Ingram, George Chesebro. *Producer* Sigmund Neufeld *Director* Sam Newfield *Original Screenplay* Oliver Drake, Elizabeth Beecher *Music* Johnny Lange, Lew Porter.
© Producers Releasing Corp., 10 February 1942; LP11140.

The Lone Rider in "Death Rides the Plains." © 1943. 6 reels, sd. (R) April 30, 1943. 57 mins. ("Lone Rider" series.) *With* Bob Livingston, Al St. John, Nica Doret, Ray Bennett, I. Stanford Jolley, Kermit Maynard, George Chesebro, John Elliott, Slim Whitaker, Karl Hackett, Frank Ellis, Ted Mapes, Dan White, Jimmy Aubrey. *Producer* Sigmund Neufeld *Director* Sam Newfield Original Story Patricia Harper *Screenplay* Joe O'Donnell *Music Director* David Chudnow *Film Editor* Holbrook N. Todd.
© Producers Releasing Corp., 15 May 1943; LP12054.

The Lone Rider in Frontier Fury. © 1941. 6 reels, sd. (R) August 8, 1941. 62 mins. ("Lone Rider" series.) *With* George Houston, Al St. John, Hillary Brooke, Karl Hackett, Ted Adams, Archie Hill, Budd Buster, Virginia Card, Edward Piel, Sr., John Elliott, Tom London, Frank Ellis, Dan White, Horace B. Carpenter, Tex Cooper, Tex Palmer, Curley Dresden, Wally West, Herman Hack. *Producer* Sigmund Neufeld *Director* Sam Newfield *Original Screenplay* Fred Myton *Music* Johnny Lange, Lew Porter *Film Editor* Holbrook N. Todd.
© Producers Releasing Corp., 10 May 1941; LP10487.

The Lone Rider in Ghost Town. © 1941. 6 reels, sd. (R) May 16, 1941. 64 mins. ("Lone Rider" series.) *With* George Houston, Al St. John, Alaine Brandes, Budd Buster, Frank Hagney, Alden Chase, Reed Howes, Charles King, George Chesebro, Edward Piel, Sr., Archie Hall, Jay Wilsey (Buffalo Bill, Jr.), Karl Hackett, Don Forrest, Frank Ellis, Curley Dresden, Steve Clark, Byron Vance, Jack Ingram, Augie Gomez, Lane Bradford. *Producer* Sigmund Neufeld *Director* Sam Newfield *Original Screenplay* Joe O'Donnell *Film Editor* Holbrook N. Todd.
© Producers Releasing Corp., 10 May 1941; LP10487.

The Lone Rider in "Law of the Saddle." © 1943. 6 reels, sd. (R) August 28, 1943. 57 mins. Presented by PRC Pictures Corp. ("Lone Rider" series.) *With* Bob Livingston, Al St. John, Betty Miles, Lane Chandler, John Elliott, Reed Howes, Curley Dresden, Al Ferguson, Frank Ellis, Frank Hagney, Jimmy Aubrey. *Producer* Sigmund Neufeld *Director* Melville DeLay *Original Story and Screenplay* Fred Myton *Film Editor* Holbrook N. Todd.
© Producers Releasing Corp., 18 September 1943; LP12265.

The Lone Rider in "Overland Stagecoach." (R) December 11, 1942. 58 mins. ("Lone Rider" series.) *With* Bob Livingston, Al St. John, Smoky (Dennis) Moore, Julie Duncan, Glenn Strange, Charles King, Art Mix, Budd Buster, Ted Adams, Julian Rivero, John Elliott, Tex Cooper. *Producer* Sigmund Neufeld *Director* Sam Newfield *Screenplay* Steve Braxton (Sam Robins) *Music* Leo Erdody *Film Editor* Holbrook N. Todd.
© Producers Releasing Corp., 8 February 1943; LP11843.

The Lone Rider in "Raiders of Red Gap." © 1943. 6 reels, sd. (R) September 30, 1943. 54 mins. ("Lone Rider" series.) *With* Bob Livingston, Al St. John, Myrna Dell, Ed Cassidy, Charles King, Slim Whitaker, Kermit Maynard, Roy Brent, Frank Ellis, George Chesebro, Bud Osborne, Jimmy Aubrey, Merrill McCormack, George Morrell, Wally West, Reed Howes. *Producer* Sigmund Neufeld *Director* Sam Newfield *Screenplay* Joseph O'Donnell.
© PRC Pictures, Inc., 10 October 1943; LP12311.

The Lone Rider in Texas Justice. © 1942. 6 reels, sd. (R) June 12, 1942. 60 mins. ("Lone Rider" series.) *With* George Houston, Al St. John, Dennis Moore, Wanda McKay, Claire Rochelle, Archie Hall, Slim Whitaker, Edward Piel, Sr., Karl Hackett, Julian Rivero, Curley Dresden, Dirk Thane, Horace B. Carpenter, Steve Clark, Frank Ellis, Merrill McCormack, Ray Jones. *Producer* Sigmund Neufeld *Director* Sam Newfield *Original Screenplay* Steve Braxton *Music* Johnny Lange, Lew Porter *Film Editor* Holbrook N. Todd.
© Producers Releasing Corp., 1 June 1942; LP11342.

The Lone Rider in "Wild Horse Rustlers." © 1943. 6 reels, sd., 35 mm. (R) February 21, 1943. Presented by Producers Releasing Corp. ("Lone Rider" series.) *With* Bob Livingston, Al St. John, Linda Johnson, Lane Chandler, Stanley Price, Frank Ellis, Karl Hackett, Jimmy Aubrey, Kansas Moehring, Silver Harr. *Producer* Sigmund Neufeld *Director* Sam Newfield *Original Screenplay* Steve Braxton (Sam Robins) *Music* Leo Erdody *Film Editor* Holbrook N. Todd. *Appl. Author* PRC Pictures, Inc.
© Producers Releasing Corp., 10 February 1943; LP530.

The Lone Rider in "Wolves of the Range." © 1943. 6 reels, sd. (R) June 21, 1943. 60 mins. ("Lone Rider" series.) *With* Bob Livingston, Al St. John, Frances Gladwin, I. Stanford Jolley, Karl Hackett, Ed Cassidy, Jack Ingram, Kenne Duncan, Budd Buster, Robert Hill, Slim Whitaker, Jack Holmes, Roy Bucko. *Producer* Sigmund Neufeld *Director* Sam Newfield *Original Story and Screenplay* Joe O'Donnell *Film Editor* Holbrook N. Todd.
© Producers Releasing Corp., 18 June 1943; LP12099.

Kay Aldridge attempts to influence the law (top) and shows she is not to be trifled with (bottom) in "The Man Who Walked Alone."

The Lone Rider Rides On. © 1941. 6 reels, sd. (R) January 10, 1941. 61 mins. ("Lone Rider" series.) *With* George Houston, Al St. John, Hillary Brooke, Lee Powell, Buddy Roosevelt, Al Bridge, Frank Hagney, Tom London, Karl Hackett, Forrest Taylor, Frank Ellis, Curley Dresden, Isabel LaMal, Harry Harvey, Jr., Don Forrest, Bob Kortman, Wally West, Steve Clark. *Producer* Sigmund Neufeld *Director* Sam Newfield *Original Screenplay* Joseph O'Donnell *Editor* Holbrook N. Todd.
© Producers Releasing Corp., 8 January 1941; LP10156.

Machine Gun Mama. © 1944. 7 reels, sd. (R) August 18, 1944. 67 mins. *With* Armida, El Brendel, Luis Alberni. *Producer* Jack Schwarz *Director* Harold M. Young *Original Screenplay* Sam Newman *Music Arrangers* Mort Glickman, David Chudnow *Film Editor* Robert O. Crandall.
© PRC Pictures, Inc., 8 February 1944; LP13582.

The Mad Monster. © 1942. 8 reels, sd. (R) May 15, 1942. 79 mins. *With* Johnny Downs, Anne Nagel. *Producer* Sigmund Neufeld *Director* Sam Newfield *Original Screenplay* Fred Myton *Music* David Chudnow *Film Editor* Holbrook N. Todd.
© Producers Releasing Corp., 7 May 1942; LP11286.

Man of Courage. © 1943. 7 reels, sd. (R) January 4, 1943. 67 mins. *With* Barton MacLane, Charlotte Wynters, Lyle Talbot, Dorothy Burgess, Patsy Nash, Forrest Taylor, John Ince, Jane Novack, Erskine Johnson, Claire Grey, Steve Clark, Billy Gray, Frank Yaconelli. *Producer* Lester Cutler *Associate Producer* C.A. Beute *Director* Alexis Thurn-Taxis *Authors* Barton MacLane, Herman Ruby, Lew Pollack *Screenplay* Arthur St. Claire, Barton MacLane, John Vlahos *Musical Director* Lee Zahler *Cameraman* Marcel LePicard *Film Editor* Fred Bain.
© Producers Releasing Corp., 30 January 1943; LP11816.

The Man Who Walked Alone. © 1945. 7 reel, sd. (R) March 15, 1945. 65 mins. *With* Kay Aldridge, Dave O'Brien, Walter Catlett, Guinn "Big Boy" Williams. *Producer* Leon Fromkess *Direction and Original Story* Christy Cabanne *Screenplay* Robert Lee Johnson *Film Editor* W. Donn Hayes.
© PRC Pictures, Inc., 15 March 1945; LP13577.

Marked for Murder. © 1945. 6 reels, sd. (R) February 8, 1945. 56 mins. An Alexander-Stern Production. ("Texas Rangers" series.) *With* Tex Ritter, Dave O'Brien, Guy Wilkerson, Marilyn McConnell, Henry Hall, Edward Cassidy, Charles King, Jack Ingram, Bob Kortman, Wen Wright, The Milo Twins, Kermit Maynard. *Producer* Arthur Alexander *Direction and Original Screenplay* Elmer Clifton *Music Director* Lee Zahler *Photographer* Edward Kull *Film Editor* Holbrook N. Todd.
© PRC Pictures, Inc. 8 February 1945; LP13560.

Marked Men. © 1940. 7 reels, sd. (R) August 28, 1940. 66 mins. *With* Warren Hull, Isabel Jewell. *Producer* Sigmund Neufeld *Director* Sherman Scott (Sam Newfield) *Original Story* Harold Greene *Screenplay* George Bricker *Music Director* David Chudnow *Cameraman* Jack Greenhalgh *Film Editor* Holbrook N. Todd.
© Producers Releasing Corp., 28 August 1940; LP9880.

The Mask of Diijon. © 1946. 8 reels, sd. (R) March 7, 1946. 74 mins. Presented by PRC Pictures. *With* Erich von Stroheim, Jeanne Bates. *Producers* Max Alexander, Alfred Stern *Director* Lew Landers *Original Story* Arthur St. Claire *Screenplay* Arthur St. Claire, Griffin Jay.
© Pathe Industries, Inc., 1 March 1946; LP130.

Men of San Quentin. © 1942. 8 reels, sd. (R) May 22, 1942. 78 mins. *With* Anthony Hughes, George Breakston. *Producers* Martin Mooney, Max King *Director* William Beaudine *Original Story* Martin Mooney *Screenplay* Ernest Booth *Film Editor* Dan Milner.
© Producers Releasing Corp., 12 May 1942; LP11287.

Men of the Sea. © 1944. 5 reels, sd. (R) April 30, 1944. 48 mins. Released by PRC Pictures, Inc. A G.H.W. Production. *With* Wilfred Lawson, Mary Jerrold. *Director* Norman Walker *Story* Manning Haynes *Scenario* Harold Simpson *Continuity* Phyllis Crocker *Music Director* Albert Cazabon *Photographer* Eric Cross *Editor* Sam Simmonds.
© PRC Pictures, Inc., 30 April 1944; LP12625.

Men on Her Mind. © 1944. 8 reels, sd. (R) February 12, 1944. 67 mins. *With* Mary Beth Hughes, Edward Norris. *Producer* Alfred Stern *Director* Wallace W. Fox *Original Screenplay* Raymond L. Schrock *Music Director* Lee Zahler *Film Editor* Charles Henkel, Jr.
© PRC Pictures, Inc., 2 December 1944; LP13584.

Mercy Plane. (R) December 4, 1939. 72 mins. (Producers Distributing Corp.) *With* James Dunn, Frances Gifford. *Director* Richard Harlan.

Minstrel Man. © 1944. 8 reels, sd., 35 mm. (R) August 1, 1944. 69 mins. *With* Benny Fields, Gladys George. *Producer* Leon Fromkess *Director* Joseph H. Lewis *Original Story* Martin Mooney, Raymond L. Schrock *Screenplay* Irwin R. Franklyn, Pierre Gendron *Music Score* Ferde Grofé *Music Director* Leo Erdody.
© PRC Pictures, Inc., 30 June 1944; LP428.

The Miracle Kid. © 1941. 7 reels, sd. (R) November 14, 1941. 69 mins. *With* Tom Neal, Carol Hughes. *Producer* John T. Coyle *Director* William Beaudine *Original Story from an idea by* Henry Sucher *Screenplay* Gerald D. Adams, Henry Sucher, John T. Coyle *Music Director* Clarence Wheeler *Film Editor* Guy V. Thayer, Jr.
© Producers Releasing Corp., 27 October 1941; LP10822.

Misbehaving Husbands. © 1940. 7 reels, sd. (R) December 20, 1940. 65 mins. *With* Harry Langdon, Ralph Byrd. *Producer* Jed Buell *Director* William Beaudine *Original Story* Cea Sabin *Screenplay* Vernon Smith, Claire Parrish *Film Editor* Robert Crandall.
© Producers Releasing Corp., 13 December 1940; LP10164.

Miss V. from Moscow. © 1942. 7 reels, sd. (R) November 23, 1942. 71 mins. An M&H Production. *With* Lola Lane, Noel Madison, Howard Banks, Paul Weigel, John Vosper, Anna Demetrio, William Vaughn, Juan De La Cruz,

Hugh Beaumont (left), Cheryl Walker, a bespectacled Regis Toomey, and an unbilled but obviously distressed female player in "Murder Is My Business."

Kathryn Sheldon, Victor Kendell, Richard Kipling. *Producer* George Merrick *Director* Albert Herman *Author* Arthur St. Claire *Screenplay* Arthur St. Claire, Sherman Lowe *Music Director* Lee Zahler *Cameraman* Marcel LePicard *Editor* W.L. Brown.
© Producers Releasing Corp., 4 November 1942; LP11681.

The Missing Corpse. © 1945. 6 reels, sd. (R) June 1, 1945. 62 mins. *With* J. Edward Bromberg, Frank Jenks. *Producer* Leon Fromkess *Director* Albert Herman *Screenplay* Ray Schrock *Music* Karl Hajos *Film Editor* W. Donn Hayes. From a story by Harry O. Hoyt.
© PRC Pictures, Inc., 6 June 1945; LP13657.

Mr. Celebrity. © 1941. 7 reels, sd. Producers Releasing Corp. *With* Robert "Buzzy" Henry, Francis X. Bushman, Clara Kimball Young, Jim Jeffries. *Producer* Martin Mooney *Director* William Beaudine *Original Story* Martin Mooney, Charles Samuels *Screenplay* Martin Mooney *Film Editor* Robert Crandall.
© Producers Releasing Corporation, 8 October 1941; LP10911.

The Monster Maker. © 1944. 7 reels, sd. (R) April 15, 1944. 62 mins. *With* J. Carroll Naish, Ralph Morgan. *Producer* Sigmund Neufeld *Director* Sam Newfield *Original Story* Lawrence Williams *Screenplay* Pierre Gendron, Martin Mooney *Music Score* Albert Glasser *Film Editor* Holbrook N. Todd.
© PRC Pictures, Inc., 15 April 1944; LP13611.

Murder Is My Business. © 1946. 7 reels, sd. (R) April 10, 1946. 63 mins. Presented by PRC Pictures. *With* Hugh Beaumont, Cheryl Walker. *Producer* Sig-

mund Neufeld *Director* Sam Newfield *Screenplay* Fred Myton *Music Director* Leo Erdody *Film Editor* Holbrook N. Todd. Based upon original characters and story by Brett Halliday. *Appl. Author* PRC Pictures, Inc.
© Pathe Industries, Inc., 18 June 1946; LP385.

My Son, the Hero. © 1943. 7 reels, sd. (R) April 5, 1943. 66 mins. *With* Patsy Kelly, Roscoe Karns, Joan Blair, Carol Hughes, Maxie Rosenbloom, Luis Alberni, Joseph Allen, Jr., Lois Collier, Jennie Le Gon, Nick Stewart, Hal Price, Al St. John, Elvira Gurcy, Isabel La Mal, Maxine Leslie. *Producer* Peter Van Duinen *Director* Edgar G. Ulmer *Screenplay* Edgar G. Ulmer, Doris Malloy *Cameraman* Jack Greenhalgh, Robert Cline *Music Score* Leo Erdody *Editor* Charles Henkel, Jr.
© Producers Releasing Corp., 23 March 1943; LP11933.

The Mysterious Rider. See **Billy the Kid in "The Mysterious Rider."**

Nabonga (Gorilla). © 1944. 7 reels, sd. (R) January 25, 1944. 73 mins. *With* Buster Crabbe, Fifi D'Orsay. *Producer* Sigmund Neufeld *Director* Sam Newfield *Original Story and Screenplay* Fred Myton *Music Score* Willy Stahl *Film Editor* Holbrook N. Todd.
© PRC Pictures, Inc., 30 January 1944; LP2467.

Navajo Kid. © 1945. 6 reels, sd. (R) November 21, 1945. 59 mins. *With* Bob Steele, Syd Saylor, Edward Cassidy, Caren Marsh, Stanley Blystone, Edward Howard, Charles King, Bud Osborne, Budd Buster, Henry Hall, Gertrude Glorie, Bert Dillard, Rex Rossi. *Producer* Arthur Alexander *Direction and Original Screenplay* Harry Fraser *Music Director* Lee Zahler *Photographer* Jack Greenhalgh *Film Editor* Roy Livingston.
© PRC Pictures, Inc., 8 December 1945; LP13700.

Nazi Spy Ring. See **The Dawn Express.**

A Night for Crime. © 1942. 8 reels, sd. (R) February 18, 1943. *With* Glenda Farrell, Lyle Talbot. *Producer* Lester Cutler *Director* Alexis Thurn-Taxis *Original Story* Jimmy Starr *Screenplay* Arthur St. Claire, Sherman Lowe *Music Director* Lee Zahler *Film Editor* Fred Bain.
© Producers Releasing Corp., 12 February 1942; LP11769.

Oath of Vengeance. © 1944. 6 reels, sd. (R) December 9, 1944. 57 mins. ("Billy Carson" series.) *With* Buster Crabbe, Al St. John, Mady Lawrence, Jack Ingram, Charles King, Marin Sais, Karl Hackett, Kermit Maynard, Hal Price, Frank Ellis, Budd Buster, Jimmy Aubrey. *Producer* Sigmund Neufeld *Director* Sam Newfield *Original Story and Screenplay* Fred Myton.
© PRC Pictures, Inc., 9 December 1944; LP13576.

Out of the Night. (Strange Illusion). © 1945. 9 reels, sd. (R) March 31, 1945. 87 mins. *With* Jimmy Lydon, Sally Eilers. *Producer* Leon Fromkess *Director* Edgar G. Ulmer *Screenplay* Adele Commandini. Based on an original story by Fritz Rotter.
© PRC Pictures, Inc., 31 March 1945; LP13567.

Outlaw Roundup. © 1944. 6 reels, sd. (R) February 10, 1944. 55 mins. ("Texas Ranger" series) *With* Dave O'Brien, Jim Newill, Guy Wilkerson, Helen

Chapman, Jack Ingram, Reed Howes, I. Stanford Jolley, Charles King, Bud Osborne, Frank Ellis, Budd Buster, Frank McCarroll, Jimmy Aubrey. *Producer* Alfred Stern *Director* Harry Fraser *Original Screenplay* Elmer Clifton *Music Director* Lee Zahler *Photographer* Ira Morgan *Film Editor* Charles Henkel, Jr.
    © PRC Pictures, Inc., 2 February 1944; LP12475.

Outlaws of Boulder Pass. © 1943. 6 reels, sd. (R) November 28, 1942. ("Lone Rider" series.) *With* George Houston, Al St. John, Dennis Moore, Marjorie Manners, Charles King, I. Stanford Jolley, Karl Hackett, Ted Adams, Kenne Duncan, Frank Ellis, Steve Clark, Jimmy Aubrey, Budd Buster. *Producer* Sigmund Neufeld *Director* Sam Newfield *Screenplay* Steve Braxton (Sam Robins) *Music* Johnny Lang, Lew Porter *Film Editor* Holbrook N. Todd.

Outlaws of the Plains. © 1946. 6 reels, sd., 35mm. (R) September 22, 1946. 56 mins. ("Billy Carson" series.) *With* Buster Crabbe, Al St. John, Patti McCarty, Charles King, Karl Hackett, Jack O'Shea, John L. "Bob" Cason, Bud Osborne, Budd Buster, Roy Brent, Charles "Slim" Whitaker. *Producer* Sigmund Neufeld *Director* Sam Newfield *Original Story* Elmer Clifton *Screenplay* A. Fredric Evans *Music Director* Lee Zahler *Film Editor* Holbrook N. Todd.
    © Pathe Industries, Inc., 22 September 1946; LP578.

Outlaws of the Rio Grande. © 1941. 6 reels, sd. (R) March 7, 1941. 63 mins. *With* Tim McCoy, Virginia Carpenter, George Chesebro, Philip Turich, Charles King, Ralph Peters, Rex Lease, Kenne Duncan, Karl Hackett, Frank Ellis, Thornton Edwards, Joe Dominguez, Sherry Tansey. *Producer* Sigmund Neufeld *Director* Peter Stewart (Sam Newfield) *Original Screenplay* George H. Plympton *Editor* Holbrook N. Todd.
    © Producers Releasing Corp., 5 March 1941; LP10302.

Overland Riders. © 1946. 6 reels, sd., 35 mm. (R) August 21, 1946. 54 mins. Presented by PRC Pictures, Inc. ("Billy Carson" series.) *With* Buster Crabbe, Al St. John, Patti McCarty, Slim Whitaker, Bud Osborne, Jack O'Shea, Frank Ellis, Al Ferguson, John L. "Bob" Cason, George Chesebro, Lane Bradford, Wally West. *Producer* Sigmund Neufeld *Director* Sam Newfield *Original Story and Screenplay* Ellen Coyle *Music Director* Lee Zahler *Film Editor* Holbrook N. Todd. *Appl. Author* PRC Pictures, Inc.
    © Pathe Industries, Inc., 21 August 1946; LP531.

Overland Stagecoach. See The Lone Rider in "Overland Stagecoach."

The Panther's Claw. © 1942. 8 reels, sd. (R) April 17, 1942. 70 mins. *With* Sidney Blackmer, Lynn Starr. *Producer* Lester Cutler *Director* William Beaudine *Original Story* Anthony Abbott *Screenplay* Martin Mooney *Film Editor* Fred Bain.
    © Producers Releasing Corp., 3 March 1942; LP11184.

Paper Bullets. © 1941. 8 reels, sd. (R) June 13, 1941. 72 mins. *With* Joan Woodbury, Jack La Rue. *Producer* Maurice Kozinsky *Director* Phil Rosen *Original Story and Screenplay* Martin Mooney *Music Direction* Johnny Lange, Lew Porter *Cinematographer* Arthur Martinelli *Film Editor* Martin G. Cohn.
    © Producers Releasing Corp., 6 June 1941; LP10576.

Byron Foulger (top, center) doesn't look too pleased at being in the lineup, while Lynn Starr (bottom) doesn't look too pleased with Sidney Blackmer in these scenes from "The Panther's Claw."

The Payoff. © 1943. 8 reels, sd. (R) January 21, 1943. 74 mins. *With* Lee Tracy, Tina Thayer. *Producer* Jack Schwarz *Director* Arthur Dreifuss *Original Story* Arthur Hoerl *Screenplay* Edward Dein *Music Score* Charles Dant *Film Editor* Charles Henkel, Jr.
  © Producers Releasing Corp., 30 January 1943; LP11817.

Phantom of 42nd Street. © 1945. 6 reels, sd. (R) May 2, 1945. 58 mins. *With* Dave O'Brien, Kay Aldridge. *Associate Producers* Martin Mooney, Albert Herman *Director* Albert Herman *Screenplay* Milton Raison *Music* Karl Hajos *Film Editor* Hugh Winn. Based on the novel by Jack Harvey and Milton Raison.
  © PRC Pictures, Inc., 2 May 1945; LP13570.

Philo Vance Returns. © 1947. 64 min., sd., b&w, 35 mm. (R) June 14, 1947. (Eagle-Lion Films, Inc.) *With* William Wright, Terry Austin, Leon Belasco. *Producer* Howard Welsch *Director* William Beaudine *Original Screenplay* Robert E. Kent *Music* Albert Glasser *Music Director* Irving Friedman *Film Editor* Gene Fowler, Jr.
  © Pathe Industries, Inc., 14 June 1947; LP1052.

Philo Vance's Gamble. © 1947. sd., b&w, 35 mm. (R) April 13, 1947. 62 mins. (Eagle-Lion Films, Inc.) *With* Alan Curtis, Tala Birell, Terry Austin, Frank Jenks. *Producer* Howard Welsch *Director* Basil Wrangell *Original Story* Lawrence Edmund Taylor *Screenplay* Eugene Conrad, Arthur St. Claire *Music Director* Irving Friedman *Film Editor* W. Donn Hayes.
  © Pathe Industries, Inc., 12 March 1947; LP1205.

Philo Vance's Secret Mission. © 1947. sd., b&w, 35 mm. (R) August 30, 1947. 58 mins. (Eagle-Lion Films, Inc.) *With* Alan Curtis, Sheila Ryan, Tala Birell. *Producer* Howard Welsch *Director* Reginald Le Borg *Original Screenplay* Lawrence Edmund Taylor *Film Editor* W. Donn Hayes.
  © Pathe Industries, Inc., 5 August 1947; LP1180.

The Pinto Bandit. © 1944. 6 reels, sd. (R) April 27, 1944. 56 mins. ("Texas Rangers" series.) *With* Dave O'Brien, Jim Newill, Guy Wilkerson, Mady Lawrence, James Martin, Jack Ingram, Edward Cassidy, Budd Buster, Karl Hackett, Robert Kortman, Charles King, Jimmy Aubrey. *Producer* Alfred Stern *Direction and Original Screenplay* Elmer Clifton *Music Director* Lee Zahler *Photographer* Edward Kull *Film Editor* Charles Henkel, Jr.
  © PRC Pictures, Inc., 27 April 1944; LP12618.

Pioneer Justice. © 1947. sd., b&w, 35 mm. (R) June 28, 1947. 56 mins. (Eagle-Lion Films, Inc.) *With* Lash La Rue, Al "Fuzzy" St. John, Jennifer Holt, William Fawcett, Jack Ingram, Dee Cooper, Lane Bradford, Henry Hall, Steve Drake, Bob Woodward, Terry Frost, Wally West, Slim Whitaker. *Producer* Jerry Thomas *Director* Ray Taylor *Original Screenplay* Adrian Page *Film Editor* Hugh Winn.
  © Pathe Industries, Inc., 29 May 1947; LP1133.

Prairie Badmen. © 1946. 6 reels, sd., 35 mm. (R) July 17, 1946. 55 mins. ("Billy Carson" series.) *With* Buster Crabbe, Al St. John, Patricia Knox, Charles King, Edward Cassidy, Kermit Maynard, John L. Cason, Steve Clark, Frank Ellis, Budd Buster. *Producer* Sigmund Neufeld *Director* Sam Newfield *Original*

Story and Screenplay Fred Myton *Music Director* Lee Zahler *Film Editor* Holbrook N. Todd.
© Pathe Industries, Inc., 9 July 1946; LP479.

Prairie Outlaws. © 1948. sd., b&w, 35 mm. (R) May 12, 1948. 57 mins. (Eagle-Lion Films, Inc.) *With* Eddie Dean, Roscoe Ates, Sarah Padden, Lash La Rue. *Producer and Director* Robert Emmett Tansey *Original Screenplay* Frances Kavanaugh *Film Editor* Hugh Winn.
© Pathe Industries, Inc., 12 May 1948; LP1669.

Prairie Pals. © 1943. 6 reels, sd. (R) September 4, 1942. 60 mins. *With* Bill "Cowboy Rambler" Boyd, Art Davis, Lee Powell, Charles King, Esther Estrella, John Merton, J. Merrill Holmes, Kermit Maynard, I. Stanford Jolley, Karl Hackett, Bob Burns, Al St. John, Al Taylor, Art Dillard, Curley Dresden, Frank McCarroll, Bill Patton, Carl Mathews, Frank Ellis, Jack Kinney, Morgan Flowers. *Producer* Sigmund Neufeld *Director* Peter Stewart (Sam Newfield) *Original Screenplay* Patricia Harper *Music* Johnny Lange, Lew Porter *Film Editor* Holbrook N. Todd.
© Producers Releasing Corp., 19 February 1943; LP11873.

Prairie Rustlers. © 1945. 6 reels, sd. (R) November 7, 1945. 56 mins. ("Billy Carson" series.) *With* Buster Crabbe, Al St. John, Evelyn Finley, Karl Hackett, Bud Osborne, Marin Sais, I. Stanford Jolley, Kermit Maynard, Herman Hack, George Morrell, Tex Cooper, Dorothy Vernon. *Producer* Sigmund Neufeld *Director* Sam Newfield *Original Story and Screenplay* Fred Myton *Music Director* Lee Zahler *Film Editor* Holbrook N. Todd.
© PRC Pictures, Inc., 20 November 1945; LP13560.

Prisoner of Japan. © 1942. 7 reels, sd. (R) July 22, 1942. 64 mins. Presented by Producers Releasing Corp. Atlantis Picture Corp. An Arthur Ripley Production. *With* Alan Baxter, Gertrude Michael. *Producer* Seymour Nebenzal *Director* Arthur Ripley *Original Screenplay* Robert Chapin, Arthur Ripley *Music Score* Leo Erdody *Film Editor* Holbrook Todd. Based on a story by Edgar G. Ulmer.
© Producers Releasing Corp., 3 July 1942; LP11480.

Queen of Broadway. © 1943. 7 reels, sd. (R) March 8, 1943. 62 mins. *With* Rochelle Hudson, Buster Crabbe. *Producer* Bert Sternbach *Director* Sam Newfield *Original Story* George Wallace Sayre *Screenplay* Rusty McCullough, George Wallace Sayre *Music Score* Leo Erdody *Film Editor* Holbrook N. Todd.
© Producers Releasing Corp., 26 January 1943; LP11812.

Queen of Burlesque. © 1946. 7 reels, sd. (R) July 24, 1946. 70 mins. *With* Evelyn Ankers, Carleton Young. *Director* Sam Newfield *Original Screenplay* David A. Lang. *Appl. Author* PRC Pictures, Inc.
© Pathe Industries, Inc., 4 July 1946; LP418.

Raiders of Red Gap. See The Lone Rider in "Raiders of Red Gap."

Raiders of the West. © 1942. 6 reels, sd. (R) February 13, 1942. 64 mins. *With* Bill "Cowboy Rambler" Boyd, Art Davis, Lee Powell, Virginia Carroll, Rex

Gertrude Michael is an unwilling guest of Ernest Dorian (second from left) and the Japanese government in "Prisoner of Japan."

Lease, Charles King, Glenn Strange, Slim Whitaker, Milt Kibbee, Lynton Brent, John Elliott, Eddie Dean, Curley Dresden, William Desmond, Dale Sherwood, Kenne Duncan, Bill Cody, Jr., Reed Howes, Hal Price, Fred Toones, Carl Sepulveda, Frank Ellis, John Cason. *Producer* Sigmund Neufeld *Director* Peter Stewart (Sam Newfield) *Original Screenplay* Oliver Drake *Film Editor* Holbrook N. Todd.

© Producers Releasing Corp., 15 January 1942; LP11131.

Range Beyond the Blue. © 1947. sd., b&w, 35 mm. (R) March 17, 1947. 63 mins. *With* Eddie Dean, Roscoe Ates, Helen Mowery, Bob Duncan, Ted Adams, Bill Hammond, George Turner, Ted French, Brad Slaven, Steve Clark, The Sunshine Boys, "Flash." *Producer* Jerry Thomas *Director* Ray Taylor *Original Screenplay* Patricia Harper *Film Editor* Hugh Winn.

© Pathe Industries, Inc., 17 March 1947; LP892.

The Rangers Take Over. © 1943. 6 reels, sd. (R) December 25, 1942. 60 mins. ("Texas Ranger" series.) *With* Dave "Tex" O'Brien, Jim Newill, Iris Meredith, Guy Wilkerson, Cal Shrum's Rhythm Rangers, Forrest Taylor, I. Stanford Jolley, Charles King, Carl Mathews, Harry Harvey, Lynton Brent, Bud Osborne. *Associate Producers* Alfred Stern, Arthur Alexander *Director* Albert Herman *Screenplay* Elmer Clifton *Musical Director* Lee Zahler *Cameraman* Robert Cline *Film Editor* Charles Henkel, Jr.

© Producers Releasing Corp., 30 January 1943; LP11815.

Reg'lar Fellers. © 1941. 7 reels, sd. (R) September 5, 1941. 65 mins. *With* Billy Lee, Alfalfa Switzer. *Director* Arthur Dreifuss *Original Story* Arthur Hoerl *Screenplay* Arthur Hoerl, Arthur Dreifuss, William C. Kent *Music Score* Ross DiMaggio *Film Editor* Carl Pierson. Based on the comic strip by Gene Byrnes.
    © Producers Releasing Corp., 15 August 1941; LP10785.

The Renegades. See Billy the Kid in "The Renegades."

Return of the Lash. © 1947. sd., b&w, 35 mm. (R) October 11, 1947. 53 mins. (Eagle-Lion Films, Inc.) *With* Al "Lash" La Rue, Al St. John, Mary Maynard, Brad Slaven, George Chesebro, George DeNormand, Lee Morgan, Lane Bradford, John Gibson, Dee Cooper, Carl Mathews, Bud Osborne, Slim Whitaker, Kermit Maynard, Frank Ellis, Bob Woodward. *Producer* Jerry Thomas *Director* Ray Taylor *Original Screenplay* Joseph O'Donnell, Walter Greene *Film Editor* Hugh Winn.
    © Pathe Industries, Inc., 23 July 1947; LP1251.

Return of the Rangers. © 1943. 6 reels, sd. (R) October 26, 1943. 60 mins. ("Texas Rangers" series.) *With* Dave O'Brien, Jim Newill, Guy Wilkerson, Nell O'Day, Glenn Strange, Emmett Lynn, I. Stanford Jolley, Robert Barron, Henry Hall, Harry Harvey, Dick Alexander, Charles King. *Producer* Arthur Alexander *Direction and Original Screenplay* Elmer Clifton *Music Director* Lee Zahler *Cameraman* Robert Cline *Film Editor* Charles Henkel, Jr.
    © PRC Pictures, Inc., 26 October 1943; LP13596.

Riders of Black Mountain. © 1940. 6 reels, sd. (R) November 11, 1940. 59 mins. *With* Tim McCoy, Pauline Haddon, Rex Lease, Ralph Peters, Edward Piel, Sr., George Chesebro, Dirk Thane, Carl Mathews. *Producer* Sigmund Neufeld *Director* Peter Stewart (Sam Newfield) *Original Screenplay* Joseph O'Donnell *Music Director* Lew Porter *Photography* Jack Greenhalgh *Film Editor* Holbrook N. Todd.
    © Producers Releasing Corp., 2 November 1940; LP10059.

Rodeo Rhythm. © 1941. 7 reels. (R) March 13, 1942. 72 mins. (PRC Pickup.) *With* Fred Scott, Pat Dunn, Patricia Redpath, Jack Cooper, Gloria Morse, H. "Doc" Hartley, Rovlene Smith, Vernon Brown, Landon Laird, John Frank, Roy Knapp's Rough Riders. *Producer* Leo J. McCarthy *Director* Fred Newmeyer *Original Story* Leo J. McCarthy *Screenplay* Gene Tuttle, Eugene Allen. *App. Author* Leo J. McCarthy.
    © Del Cal Theatres, Inc., 8 December 1941; LP10914.

Rogues' Gallery. © 1945. 7 reels, sd. (R) December 6, 1944. 60 mins. *With* Frank Jenks, Robin Raymond. *Producers* Donald C. McKean, Albert Herman *Director* Albert Herman *Original Screenplay* John T. Neville *Music Director* Lee Zahler *Film Editor* Fred Bain.
    © PRC Pictures, Inc., 1 January 1945; LP13558.

Rolling Down the Great Divide. © 1942. 6 reels, sd. (R) April 24, 1942. 60 mins. *With* Bill "Cowboy Rambler" Boyd, Art Davis, Lee Powell, Wanda McKay, Glenn Strange, Karl Hackett, J. Merrill Holmes, Ted Adams, Jack Ingram, John Elliott, George Chesebro, Horace B. Carpenter, Jack Roper, Curley

Dresden, Dennis Moore, Tex Palmer. *Producer* Sigmund Neufeld *Director* Peter Stewart (Sam Newfield) *Original Screenplay* George Milton *Music* Johnny Lange, Lew Porter *Film Editor* Holbrook N. Todd.
© Producers Releasing Corp., 8 April 1942; LP11299.

Romance of the West. © 1946. 6 reels, sd., color (Cinecolor). (R) March 20, 1946. 58 mins. *With* Eddie Dean, Joan Barton, Emmett Lynn, Forrest Taylor, Robert McKenzie, Jerry Jerome, Stanley Price, Chief Thunder Cloud, Don Kay Reynolds, Rocky Camron, Lee Roberts, Lottie Harrison, Don Williams, Jack Richardson, Matty Roubert, Forbes Murray, Jack O'Shea, Tex Cooper, Grace Christy, Jerry Riggio. *Director* Robert Emmett (Tansey) *Original Screenplay* Frances Kavanaugh *Music Director* Carl Hoefle *Film Editor* Hugh Winn.
© PRC Pictures, Inc., 10 February 1946; LP98.

Rustlers' Hideout. © 1944. 6 reels, sd. (R) September 2, 1944. 60 mins. ("Billy Carson" series.) *With* Buster Crabbe, Al St. John, Patti McCarty, Charles King, John Merton, Lane Chandler, Terry Frost, Hal Price, Al Ferguson, Frank McCarroll, Edward Cassidy, Bud Osborne. *Producer* Sigmund Neufeld *Director* Sam Newfield *Original Story and Screenplay* Joe O'Donnell *Film Editor* Holbrook N. Todd.
© PRC Pictures, Inc., 2 September 1944; LP13608.

The Sagebrush Family Trails West. (R) January 14, 1940. 60 mins. (PDC.) *With* Bobby Clark, Earle Hodgins, Nina Guilbert, Joyce Bryant, Minerva Urecal, Archie Hall, Kenne Duncan, Forrest Taylor, Carl Mathews, Wally West, Byron Vance, Angie Gomez. *Producer* Sigmund Neufeld *Director* Peter Stewart (Sam Newfield) *Screenplay* William Lively.

Secret Evidence. © 1941. 7 reels, sd. (R) January 31, 1941. 63 mins. *With* Marjorie Reynolds, Charles Quigley. *Producer* E.B. Derr *Director* William Nigh *Original Story* Edward Bennett *Screenplay* Brenda Cline *Film Editor* Elaine Turner.
© Producers Releasing Corp., 8 February 1941; LP10235.

Secrets of a Co-Ed. © 1943. 7 reels, sd. (R) October 26, 1942. 67 mins. *With* Otto Kruger, Tina Thayer, Rick Vallin. *Producers* Alfred Stern, Arthur Alexander *Director* Joseph H. Lewis *Original Screenplay* George W. Sayre *Music Direction* Lee Zahler *Photography* Robert Cline *Film Editor* Charles Henkel, Jr.
© Producers Releasing Corp., 30 January 1943; LP11820.

Secrets of a Sorority Girl. © 1946. 6 reels, sd., 35 mm. (R) August 15, 1946. 58 mins. Presented by PRC Pictures. An Alexander-Stern Production. *With* Mary Ware, Rick Vallin. *Producers* Max Alexander, Alfred Stern *Director* Frank Wisbar *Original Story* George Wallace Sayre *Screenplay* George Wallace Sayre, Arthur St. Claire *Music Director* Karl Hajos *Film Editor* Roy Livingston.
© Pathe Industries, Inc., 15 August 1946; LP501.

Seven Doors to Death. © 1944. 7 reels, sd. (R) August 5, 1944. 64 mins. Presented by PRC Pictures, Inc. An Alexander-Stern Production. *With* Chick Chandler, June Clyde. *Producer* Alfred Stern *Director* Elmer Clifton *Original*

June Clyde, some thugs, and a lot of jewelry are featured in a tense moment from "Seven Doors to Death."

Story Helen Kiely *Screenplay* Elmer Clifton *Music Director* Lee Zahler *Film Editor* Charles Henkel, Jr.
  © PRC Pictures, Inc., 25 July 1944; LP13620.

Shadow of Terror. © 1945. 6 reels, sd. (R) November 5, 1945. 64 mins. *With* Dick Fraser, Cy Kendall. *Director* Lew Landers *Original Story* Sheldon Leonard *Screenplay* Arthur St. Claire *Music Director* Karl Hajos.
  © PRC Pictures, Inc., 5 November 1945; LP415.

Shadows of Death. © 1945. 6 reels, sd. (R) April 19, 1945. 60 mins. *With* Buster Crabbe, Al St. John, Donna Dax, Charles King, Karl Hackett, Edward Piel, Sr., Bob Cason, Frank Ellis, Frank McCarroll. *Producer* Sigmund Neufeld *Director* Sam Newfield *Original Story and Screenplay* Fred Myton *Film Editor* Holbrook N. Todd.
  © PRC Pictures, Inc., 19 April 1945; LP13559.

Shake Hands with Murder. © 1944. 6 reels, sd. (R) April 22, 1944. 62 mins. PRC Pictures, Inc., for American Productions, Inc. *With* Iris Adrian, Frank Jenks. *Director* Albert Herman *Original Story* Martin Mooney *Screenplay* John T. Neville *Music Director* Lee Zahler *Film Editor* George Merrick.
  © PRC Pictures, Inc., 22 April 1944; LP13591.

Sheriff of Sage Valley. © 1943. 6 reels, sd. (R) October 2, 1943. 60 mins. ("Billy the Kid" series.) *With* Buster Crabbe, Al St. John, Dave "Tex" O'Brien, Maxine Leslie, Charles King, John Merton, Kermit Maynard, Hal Price, Curley Dresden, Jack Kirk, Lynton Brent. *Producer* Sigmund Neufeld *Director* Sherman

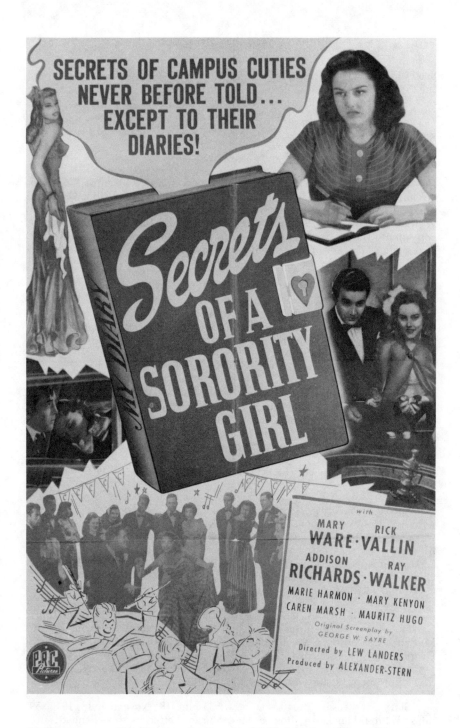

Titillating poster for "Secrets of a Sorority Girl" played up the co-ed mystique.

Scott (Sam Newfield) *Screenplay* George W. Sayre. *Appl. Author* PRC Pictures, Inc.
© Producers Releasing Corp., 1 February 1943; LP11821.

The Silver Fleet. (R) July 1, 1945. 81 mins. (Brit., PRC Pickup). *With* Ralph Richardson.

Shootin' Irons. See **West of Texas.**

Six Gun Man. © 1946. 6 reels. (R) February 1, 1946. 59 mins. *With* Bob Steele, Syd Saylor, Jean Carlin, I. Stanford Jolley, Brooke Temple, Bud Osborne, Budd Buster, Jimmie Martin, Stanley Blystone, Roy Brent, Steve Clark, Dorothy Whitmore, Ray Jones. *Producer* Arthur Alexander *Direction and Original Screenplay* Harry Fraser *Music Director* Lee Zahler *Photographer* Jack Greenhalgh *Film Editor* Roy Livingston. *Appl. Author* PRC Pictures, Inc.
© Pathe Industries, Inc., 21 June 1946; LP398.

Song of Old Wyoming. © 1945. 7 reels, sd., color (Cinecolor) (R) November 12, 1945. 65 mins. *With* Eddie Dean, Jennifer Holt, Sarah Padden, Al "Lash" La Rue, Emmett Lynn, Ray Elder, John Carpenter, Ian Keith, Robert Barron, Horace Murphy, Pete Natchenaro, Rocky Camron, Bill Bovett, Richard Cramer, Steve Clark. *Director* Robert Emmett (Tansey) *Original Screenplay* Frances Kavanaugh.
© PRC Pictures, Inc., 4 November 1945; LP13580.

South of Panama. © 1941. 7 reels, sd. (R) May 2, 1941. 68 mins. *With* Roger Pryor, Virginia Vale. *Producer* T.H. Richmond *Director* Jean Yarbrough *Original Story and Screenplay* Ben Roberts, Sidney Sheldon *Music Director* Alberto Columbo *Film Editor* Guy Thayer, Jr.
© Producers Releasing Corp., 24 April 1941; LP10577.

Spell of Amy Nugent. (R) February 10, 1945. 63 mins. *With* Derek Farr, Vera Lindsay.

Spook Town. © 1944. 6 reels, sd. (R) June 3, 1944. 59 mins. ("Texas Ranger" series.) *With* Dave O'Brien, Jim Newill, Guy Wilkerson, Mady Lawrence, Dick Curtis, Harry Harvey, Edward Cassidy, Charles King, Robert Barron, Dick Alexander, John Cason. *Producer* Arthur Alexander *Direction and Original Screenplay* Elmer Clifton *Music Director* Lee Zahler *Photographer* Robert C. Cline *Film Editor* Charles Henkel, Jr.
© PRC Pictures, Inc., 3 June 1944; LP13597.

Stagecoach Outlaws. © 1945. 6 reels, sd. (R) August 17, 1945. 59 mins. ("Billy Carson" series.) *With* Buster Crabbe, Al St. John, Frances Gladwin, Kermit Maynard, Ed Cassidy, I. Stanford Jolley, Bob Cason, Bob Kortman, Steve Clark, George Chesebro, Hank Bell. *Producer* Sigmund Neufeld *Director* Sam Newfield *Original Story and Screenplay* Fred Myton *Film Editor* Holbrook N. Todd.
© PRC Pictures, Inc., 17 August 1945; LP13578.

Stars Over Texas. © 1946. sd., b&w, 35 mm. (R) November 18, 1946. 59 mins. *With* Eddie Dean, Roscoe Ates, Shirley Patterson, Lee Bennett, Lee Roberts, Kermit Maynard, Jack O'Shea, Hal Smith, Matty Roubert, Carl Mathews, William Fawcett, The Sunshine Boys, "Flash." *Producer and Director*

Robert Emmett Tansey *Original Screenplay* Frances Kavanaugh *Film Editor* Hugh Winn.
© Pathe Industries, Inc., 18 November 1946; LP734.

Stepchild. © 1947. sd., b&w, 35mm., 70 mins. PRC Pictures, Inc. *With* Brenda Joyce, Donald Woods *Associate Producer* Jerry Briskin *Director* James Flood *Original Story* Jules Levine *Screenplay* Karen De Wolf *Music* Mario Silva *Music Director* Irving Friedman *Film Editor* W. Donn Hayes.
© Pathe Industries, Inc., 7 June 1947; LP1057.

Strange Holiday. © 1945. 6 reels, sd. (R) September 2, 1946. 56 mins. Elite Pictures. (PRC Pickup). *With* Claude Rains, Barbara Bates. *Producers* A.W. Hackel, Edward Finney, Max King *Written and Directed by* Arch Oboler *Original Music Score* Gordon Jenkins *Photographer* Robert Surtees *Editor* Fred Feitshans, Jr.
© Elite Pictures, 30 July 1945; LP13475.

Strange Illusion. See Out of the Night.

The Strangler. © 1941. 7 reels, sd. (R) April 3, 1942. 64 mins. *With* Judy Campbell, Sebastian Shaw. *Producer* Walter C. Mycroft *Director* Harold Huth *Screenplay* J. Lee Thompson, Lesley Storm *Photographer* Claude Friese-Greene *Film Editor* Flora Newton.
© Producers Releasing Corp., 28 December 1941; LP11055.

Strangler of the Swamp. © 1946. 6 reels, sd. (R) January 1, 1946. 60 mins. *With* Rosemary La Planche, Robert Barrett. *Direction and Screenplay* Frank Wisbar *Original Story* Frank Wisbar, Leo McCarthy.
© PRC Pictures, Inc., 6 January 1946; LP12.

Submarine Base. © 1943. 7 reels, sd. (R) July 20, 1943. 65 mins. *With* John Litel, Alan Baxter, Eric Blore, George Metaxa, George Lee, Rafael Storm, Fifi D'Orsay, Iris Adrian, Jacqueline Dalya, Anna Demetrio, Luis Alberni, Lucien Prival. *Producer* Jack Schwarz *Associate Producer* Harry D. Edwards *Director* Albert Kelley *Authors* Arthur St. Clair, George Merrick *Musical Composer-Director* Charles Dant *Art Director* Frank Sylos *Cameraman* Marcel LePicard *Editor* Holbrook N. Todd.
© Producers Releasing Corp., 20 July 1943; LP13592.

Suspected Person. © (R) (PRC British Pickup.) November 29, 1943. 78 mins. *With* Clifford Evans, Patricia Roc.

Swamp Woman. © 1941. 7 reels, sd. (R) December 5, 1941. 68 mins. *With* Ann Corio, Jack LaRue, Jay Novello, Richard Deane, Ian MacDonald, Mary Hull. *Producers* George M. Merrick, Max Alexander *Director* Elmer Clifton *Original Story* Fred McConnell *Screenplay* Arthur G. Durlam *Photographer* Eddie Linden *Film Editor* Charles Henkel, Jr.
© Producers Releasing Corp., 12 November 1941; LP10947.

Swing Hostess. © 1944. 8 reels, sd. (R) September 8, 1944. 76 mins. *With* Martha Tilton, Iris Adrian. *Producer* Sam Neufeld *Director* Sam Newfield

Robert Barrett (right) is the young man who wants to save Rosemary La Planche in "Strangler of the Swamp."

Original Story and Screenplay Louise Rousseau, Gail Davenport *Music Director* David Chudnow *Film Editor* Holbrook N. Todd.
© PRC Pictures, Inc., 8 September 1944; LP13563.

Terror House. © (R) April 19, 1943. 65 mins. (PRC British Pickup.) *With* Wilfred Lawson, James Mason.

Terrors on Horseback. © 1946. 6 reels, sd., 35 mm. (R) August 14, 1946. 55 mins. Presented by PRC Pictures, Inc. ("Billy Carson" series.) *With* Buster Crabbe, Al St. John, Patti McCarty, I. Stanford Jolley, Kermit Maynard, Henry Hall, Karl Hackett, Marin Sais, Budd Buster, Steve Darrell, Steve Clark, Bud Osborne, Al Ferguson, George Chesebro, Frank Ellis, Jack Kirk, Lane Bradford. *Producer* Sigmund Neufeld *Director* Sam Newfield *Original Story and Screenplay* George Milton *Music Director* Lee Zahler *Film Editor* Holbrook N. Todd.
© Pathe Industries, Inc., 14 August 1946; LP491.

Texas Manhunt. © 1942. 6 reels, sd. (R) January 2, 1942. 60 mins. *With* Bill "Cowboy Rambler" Boyd, Art Davis, Lee Powell, Julie Duncan, Dennis Moore, Frank Hagney, Karl Hackett, Frank Ellis, Arno Frey, Eddie Phillips, Kenne Duncan. *Producer* Sigmund Neufeld *Director* Peter Stewart (Sam Newfield) *Original Screenplay* William Lively *Music* Johnny Lange, Lew Porter *Film Editor* Holbrook N. Todd.
© PRC Pictures, Inc., 8 December 1942; LP13689.

The Texas Marshal. © 1941. 6 reels, sd. (R) July 13, 1941. 62 mins. *With* Tim McCoy, Art Davis and his Rhythm Riders, Kay Leslie, Karl Hackett, Edward Piel, Sr., Charles King, Dave O'Brien, Budd Buster, John Elliott, Wilson Edwards, Byron Vance, Frank Ellis. *Producer* Sigmund Neufeld *Director* Peter Stewart (Sam Newfield) *Original Screenplay* William Lively *Film Editor* Holbrook N. Todd.
© Producers Releasing Corp., 26 May 1941; LP10486.

Texas Renegades. January 17, 1940. 59 mins. (PRC.) *With* Tim McCoy, Nora Lane, Harry Harvey, Kenne Duncan, Lee Prather, Earl Gunn, Hal Price, Joe McGuinn, Edward Cassidy. *Producer* Sigmund Neufeld *Director* Peter Stewart (Sam Newfield) *Screenplay* Joseph O'Donnell.

They Raid By Night: A Story of the Commandos. © 1942. 7 reels, sd. (R) June 26, 1942. 72 mins. *With* Lyle Talbot, June Duprez, Victor Varconi. *Producer* David Harwin *Director* Spencer Gordon Bennet *Original Screenplay* Jack Natteford *Music Score* David Chudnow *Film Editor* Charles Henkel, Jr.
© Producers Releasing Corp., 15 June 1942; LP11379.

Three in the Saddle. © 1945. 6 reels, sd. (R) July 26, 1945. 61 mins. ("Texas Rangers" series.) *With* Dave O'Brien, Tex Ritter, Guy Wilkerson, Lorraine Miller, Charles King, Edward Howard, Edward Cassidy, Bud Osborne, Frank Ellis. *Producer* Arthur Alexander *Director* Harry Fraser *Original Screenplay* Elmer Clifton *Music Director* Lee Zahler.
© PRC Pictures, Inc., 26 June 1945; LP438.

Three on a Ticket. © 1947. sd., b&w, 35 mm. (R) April 5, 1947. 64 mins. *With* Hugh Beaumont, Cheryl Walker, Paul Bryar, Ralph Dunn, Louise Currie. *Producer* Sigmund Neufeld *Director* Sam Newfield *Screenplay* Fred Myton *Music* Emil Cadkin *Film Editor* Holbrook N. Todd. Based on story and characters created by Brett Halliday (pseud. of Davis Dresser). *Appl. Author* PRC Pictures Corp.
© Pathe Industries, Inc., 3 March 1947; LP857.

Thunder Town. © 1946. 6 reels, sd., 35 mm. (R) April 12, 1946. 57 mins. Presented by PRC Pictures, Inc. *With* Bob Steele, Syd Saylor, Ellen Hall, Bud Geary, Charles King, Edward Howard, Steve Clark, Bud Osborne, Jimmy Aubrey, Pascale Perry. *Producer* Arthur Alexander *Director* Harry Fraser *Original Screenplay* James Oliver *Music Director* Lee Zahler *Photographer* Robert Cline *Film Editor* Roy Livingston.
© Pathe Industries, Inc., 21 June 1946; LP397.

Thundering Gun Slingers. © 1944. 6 reels, sd., 35 mm. (R) March 25, 1944. 60 mins. ("Billy Carson" series.) *With* Buster Crabbe, Al St. John, Frances Gladwin, Karl Hackett, Charles King, Kermit Maynard, Jack Ingram, Budd Buster, George Chesebro. *Producer* Sigmund Neufeld *Director* Sam Newfield *Original Story and Screenplay* Fred Myton *Film Editor* Holbrook N. Todd.
© PRC Pictures, Inc., 15 March 1944; LP427.

Tiger Fangs. © 1943. 6 reels, sd. (R) September 10, 1943. 62 mins. *With* Frank Buck, Duncan Renaldo, June Duprez, Howard Banks, J. Farrell MacDonald, Arno Frey, Dan Seymour, J. Alex Havier, Pedro Regas. *Producer* Jack

It's Mona Barrie versus all these men in "Today I Hang."

Schwarz *Associate Producer* Fred McConnell *Director* Sam Newfield *Author and Screenplay* Arthur St. Claire *Music Score* Lee Zahler *Art Director* Paul Palmentola *Cameraman* Ira Morgan *Film Editor* George M. Merrick.
© PRC Pictures, Inc., 9 October 1943; LP13594.

The Tioga Kid. June 17, 1948. 54 mins. *With* Eddie Dean, Roscoe Ates, Jennifer Holt, Dennis Moore, Lee Bennett, William Fawcett, Eddie Parker, Bob Woodward, Louis J. Corbett, Terry Frost, Tex Palmer, Andy Parker and the Plainsmen, "Flash." *Producer* Jerry Thomas *Director* Ray Taylor *Screenplay* Ed Earl Repp *Music Supervisor* Dick Carruth *Film Editor* Hugh Winn.
© Pathe Industries, Inc., 12 June 1948; LP1670.

Today I Hang. © 1942. 7 reels, sd. (R) January 30, 1942. 63 mins. Presented by Producers Releasing Corp. An M&A Production. *With* Walter W. King, Mona Barrie. *Producers* Max Alexander, Alfred Stern *Directors* George M. Merrick, Oliver Drake *Original Story and Screenplay* Oliver Drake *Musical Direction* Lew Porter, Johnny Lange *Photographer* Eddie Linden *Film Editor* Charles Henkel, Jr.
© Producers Releasing Corp., 7 January 1942; LP10948.

Tomorrow We Live. © 1942. 7 reels, sd. (R) September 29, 1942. 64 mins. Presented by Producers Releasing Corp. Altantis Pictures Corp. *With* Jean Parker, Ricardo Cortez. *Producer* Seymour Nebenzal *Director* Edgar G. Ulmer *Story and Screenplay* Bert Lytton *Music Score* Leo Erdody *Editor* Dan Milner.

Too Many Winners. © 1947. sd., b&w, 35 mm. 60 min. PRC Pictures, Inc. Based on original characters and story by Brett Halliday (pseud. of Davis Dresser). *Producer* John Sutherland *Director* William Beaudine *Screenplay* John Sutherland *Adaptation* Fred Myton, Scott Darling *Music* Alvin Levin *Film Editor* Harry Reynolds.
© Pathe Industries, Inc., 24 May 1947; LP1021.

Too Many Women. © 1942. 7 reels, sd. (R) February 27, 1942. 67 mins. *With* Neil Hamilton, June Lang. *Director* Bernard B. Ray *Story and Screenplay* Eddie M. Davis *Film Editor* Carl Himm.
© Producers Releasing Corp., 21 January 1942; LP11143.

Torture Ship. (R) October 22, 1939. *With* Lyle Talbot, Jacqueline Wells, Irving Pichel. *Director* Victor Halperin. Based on the story *A Thousand Deaths* by Jack London.

The Town Went Wild. © 1944. 8 reels, sd. (R) December 15, 1944. 79 mins. A Roth-Green-Rouse Production. *With* Freddie Bartholomew, James Lydon. *Director* Ralph Murphy *Screenplay* Bernard Roth, Clarence Green, Russell Rouse *Music Director* Gerrard Carbonara *Film Editor* Thomas Neff.
© PRC Pictures, Inc., 15 December 1944; LP13008.

Trail of Terror. © 1943. 6 reels, sd. (R) September 14, 1943. 63 mins. ("Texas Rangers" series.) *With* Dave O'Brien, Jim Newill, Guy Wilkerson, Patricia Know, Jack Ingram, I. Stanford Jolley, Budd Buster, Kenne Duncan, Frank Ellis, Robert Hill, Dan White, Jimmy Aubrey, Rose Plummer, Tom Smith, Artie Ortego. *Producers* Alfred Stern, Arthur Alexander *Direction and Original Screenplay* Oliver Drake *Music Director* Lee Zahler *Photographer* Ira Morgan *Film Editor* Charles Henkel, Jr.
© Producers Releasing Corp., 7 September 1943; LP12243.

Tumbleweed Trail. © 1946. 6 reels, sd., 35 mm. (R) 57 mins. Presented by PRC Pictures, Inc. *With* Eddie Dean, Roscoe Ates, Shirley Patterson, Johnny McGovern, Bob Duncan, Ted Adams, Kermit Maynard, William Fawcett, Carl Mathews, Matty Roubert, Lee Roberts, Frank Ellis, The Sunshine Boys (M.H. Richman, J.O. Smith, A.L. Smith, Edward F. Wallace), "Flash." *Producer and Director* Robert Emmett Tansey *Original Screenplay* Frances Kavanaugh *Music Director* Karl Hajos *Film Editor* Hugh Winn.
© Pathe Industries, Inc., 28 October 1946; LP687.

Tumbleweed Trail. ©1942. 57 mins. *With* Bill "Cowboy Rambler" Boyd, Art Davis, Jack Rockwell, Lee Powell, Jack Montgomery, Marjorie Manners, Charles King, Karl Hackett, George Chesebro, Frank Hagney, Reed Howes, Curley Dresden, George Morrell, Art Dillard, Steve Clark, Dan White, Augie Gomez. *Producer* Sigmund Neufeld *Director* Peter Stewart (Sam Newfield) *Screenplay* Fred Myton.
© Producers Releasing Corp., 19 June 1942; LP11401.

The Underdog. © 1943. 7 reels, sd., 35 mm. (R) October 17, 1943. 65 mins. *With* Barton MacLane, Bobby Larson, Jan Wiley, Charlotte Wynters, Conrad Binyon, Elizabeth Valentine, Kenneth Harlan, George Anderson Hobo. *Producer* Max Alexander *Director* William Nigh *Authors* Lawrence E. Taylor,

Malvin Wald *Screenplay* Ben Lithman *Musical Director* Lee Zahler *Cameraman* Robert Cline *Editor* Charles Henkel, Jr.
© PRC Pictures, Inc., 17 October 1943; LP492.

Untamed Fury. © 1947. sd., b&w, 35 mm. (R) March 22, 1947. 65 mins. A Danches Brothers Production. *With* Gaylord Pendleton, Mikel Conrad, Leigh Whipper. *Producer and Director* Ewing Scott *Screenplay* Taylor Caven, Paul Gerard Smith *Music Score and Direction* Alexander Laszlo *Film Editor* Robert Crandall. From Ewing Scott's story "Gaitor Bait."
© Pathe Industries, Inc., 22 March 1947; LP889.

Valley of Vengeance. © 1944. 6 reels, sd. (R) May 5, 1944. 56 mins. ("Billy Carson" series.) *With* Buster Crabbe, Al St. John, Evelyn Finley, Edward Cassidy, Nora Bush, Donald Mayo, David Polonsky, Glenn Strange, Charles King, Jack Ingram, John Merton, Lynton Brent, Bud Osborne, Steve Clark. *Producer* Sigmund Neufeld *Director* Sam Newfield *Original Story and Screenplay* Joseph O'Donnell *Film Editor* Holbrook N. Todd.
© PRC Pictures, Inc., 15 May 1944; LP12647.

Waterfront. © 1944. 7 reels, sd. An Alexander Stern Production. Presented by PRC Pictures, Inc. *With* John Carradine, J. Carroll Naish. *Producer* Arthur Alexander *Director* Steve Sekely *Original Screenplay* Martin Mooney, Irwin R. Franklyn *Music Director* Lee Zahler *Film Editor* Charles Henkel, Jr.
© PRC Pictures, Inc., 27 May 1944; LP12668.

West of Texas (Shootin' Irons). © 1943. 6 reels, sd. (R) May 10, 1943. 54 mins. ("Texas Rangers" series.) *With* Dave O'Brien, Jim Newill, Guy Wilkerson, Frances Gladwin, Madilyn Hare, Robert Barron, Tom London, Jack Rockwell, Jack Ingram, Art Fowler. *Producers* Alfred Stern, Arthur Alexander *Direction and Original Screenplay* Oliver Drake *Music Director* Lee Zahler *Photographer* Ira Morgan *Film Editor* Charles Henkel, Jr.
© Producers Releasing Corp., 16 May 1943; LP12060.

West to Glory. © 1947. sd., b&w, 35 mm. (R) April 22, 1947. 61 mins. *With* Eddie Dean, Roscoe Ates, Delores Castle, Gregg Barton, Jimmie Martin, Zon Murray, Alex Montoya, Casey MacGregor, Billy Hammond, Ted French, Carl Mathews, Harry Vehar, The Sunshine Boys. *Producer* Jerry Thomas *Director* Ray Taylor *Original Screenplay* Elmer Clifton, Robert B. Churchill *Orchestration* Walter Greene *Film Editor* Joseph Gluck.
© Pathe Industries, Inc., 22 April 1947; LP951.

Western Cyclone. See Billy the Kid in Western Cyclone.

The Westward Trail. © 1947. 58 mins. sd., b&w, 35 mm. (R) March 13, 1948. 56 mins. *With* Eddie Dean, Roscoe Ates, Phyllis Planchard, Eileen Hardin, Steve Drake, Bob Duncan, Carl Mathews, Lee Morgan, Bob Woodward, Budd Buster, Charles "Slim" Whitaker, Frank Ellis, Andy Parker and the Plainsmen, "Copper." *Producer* Jerry Thomas *Director* Ray Taylor *Screenplay* Arthur Alan Miller *Music* Walter Greene *Film Editor* Hugh Winn.
© Pathe Industries, Inc., 25 October 1947; LP1526.

Pamela Blake (second from right) gets stern advice from the older generation in
"Why Girls Leave Home."

When the Lights Go on Again. © 1944. 8 reels, sd. (R) October 23, 1944. 76
mins. *With* James Lydon. *Producer* Leon Fromkess *Director* William K. Howard
Original Story Frank Craven *Screenplay* Milton Lazarus *Music Score* W. Franke
Harling *Music Supervision* David Chudnow *Film Editor* Donn Hayes.
   © PRC Pictures, Inc., 23 October 1944; LP13593.

The Whispering Skull. © 1944. 6 reels, sd. (R) December 20, 1944. ("Texas
Rangers" series.) *With* Dave O'Brien, Tex Ritter, Guy Wilkerson, Denny Burke,
I. Stanford Jolley, Henry Hall, George Morrell, Edward Cassidy, Bob Kortman,
Wen Wright. *Producer* Arthur Alexander *Director* Elmer Clifton *Screenplay*
Harry Fraser *Music Director* Lee Zahler *Photographer* Edward Kull *Film Editor*
Hugh Winn.
   © PRC Pictures, Inc., 29 December 1944; LP13565.

White Pongo. © 1945. 8 reels, sd. (R) November 2, 1945. 73 mins. *With*
Richard Fraser, Lionel Royce. *Producer* Sigmund Neufeld *Director* Sam
Newfield *Original Story and Screenplay* Raymond L. Schrock *Music Director*
Leo Erdody *Film Editor* Holbrook N. Todd.
   © PRC Pictures, Inc., 10 August 1945; LP13598.

Why Girls Leave Home. © 1945. 7 reels, sd. (R) October 9, 1945. 69 mins.
With Pamela Blake, Sheldon Leonard. *Producer* Sam Sax *Director* William
Berke *Original Story* Fanya Foss Lawrence *Screenplay* Fanya Foss Lawrence,
Bradford Ropes *Music Director* Walter Greene *Film Editor* Carl Pierson.
   © PRC Pictures, Inc., 5 November 1945; LP13590.

The Wife of Monte Cristo. © 1946. 8 reels, sd. (R) April 23, 1946. 80 mins. *With* Joh Loder, Lenore Aubert. *Director* Edgar G. Ulmer *Adaptation* Franz Rosenwald, Edgar G. Ulmer *Set Direction* Edgar G. Ulmer *Camera* Adolph Kull (Eugen Schüftan). Suggested by the novel by Alexandre Dumas. *Appl. Author* PRC Pictures, Inc.
© Pathe Industries, Inc., 18 June 1946; LP387.

Wild Country. © 1947. sd., b&w, 35 mm. (R) January 17, 1947. 55 mins. *With* Eddie Dean, Al "Fuzzy" St. John, Roscoe Ates, Peggy Wynn, Douglas Fowley, I. Stanford Jolley, Steve Clark, Henry Hall, Lee Roberts, Forrest Matthews, William Fawcett, Charles Jordan, Richard Cramer, Gus Taute, The Sunshine Boys, "Flash." *Producer* Jerry Thomas *Director* Ray Taylor *Original Screenplay* Arthur E. Orloff *Orchestration* Walter Greene *Film Editor* Hugh Winn.
© Pathe Industries, Inc., 7 January 1947; LP778.

Wild Horse Phantom. © 1944. 6 reels, sd. (R) October 28, 1944. 55 mins. ("Billy Carson" series.) *With* Buster Crabbe, Al St. John, Elaine Morey, Kermit Maynard, Budd Buster, Hal Price, Robert Meredith, Frank Ellis, Frank McCarroll, Bob Cason, John Elliott. *Producer* Sigmund Neufeld *Director* Sam Newfield *Original Story and Screenplay* George Milton *Film Editor* Holbrook N. Todd.
© PRC Pictures, Inc., 28 October 1944; LP13564.

Wild Horse Rustlers. See **The Lone Rider in "Wild Horse Rustlers."**

Wild West. © 1946. 8 reels, sd., color (Cinecolor), 35 mm. (R) December 1, 1946. 73 mins. Presented by PRC Pictures, Inc. *With* Eddie Dean, Roscoe Ates, Al La Rue, Robert "Buzzy" Henry, Sarah Padden, Louise Currie, Jean Carlin, Lee Bennett, Terry Frost, Warner Richmond, Lee Roberts, Bob Allen, Chief Yowlachie, Bob Duncan, Frank Pharr, John Bridges, Al Ferguson, Bud Osborne, "Flash." *Producer and Director* Robert Emmett Tansey *Original Screenplay* Frances Kavanaugh *Music Director* Karl Hajos *Orchestral Arrangements* Walter Greene *Film Editor* Hugh Winn.
© Pathe Industries, Inc., 1 December 1946; LP712.

Wolves of the Range. See **The Lone Rider in "Wolves of the Range."**

A Yank in Libya. © 1942. 7 reels, sd. (R) July 31, 1942. 67 mins. Presented by Producers Releasing Corp. An M&H Production. *With* Joan Woodbury, H.B. Warner, Duncan Reynaldo, Walter Woolf King, Parkyarkarkus. *Producer* George M. Merrick *Director* Albert Herman *Original Story and Screenplay* Arthur St. Claire, Sherman Lowe *Music Director* Lee Zahler *Film Editor* L.R. Brown.
© Producers Releasing Corp., 20 July 1942; LP11479.

The Yanks Are Coming. © 1943. 7 reels, sd. (R) November 9, 1942. 65 mins. *With* Maxie Rosenbloom, Mary Healy. *Producer* Lester Cutler *Director* Alexis Thurn-Taxis *Original Story* Tony Stern, Lew Pollack, Edward E. Kaye *Screen Adaptation* Arthur St. Claire, Sherman Loew *Music Director* Lee Zahler *Photography* Marcel LePicard *Film Editor* Fred Bain.
© Producers Releasing Corp., 30 January 1943; LP11819.

Bibliography

Adams, Les and Buck Rainey. *Shoot-Em-Ups: The Complete Reference Guide to Westerns of the Sound Era.* New Rochelle, N.Y.: Arlington House Publishers, 1978.

Everson, William K. *History of the Western Film.* Secaucus, N.J.: The Citadel Press, 1969.

The Library of Congress Copyright Catalogue 1912–1969 (Four Volumes). Washington, D.C.: Copyright Office, The Library of Congress.

McCarthy, Todd and Charles Flynn. *Kings of the Bs — Working within the Hollywood System: An Anthology of Film History and Criticism.* New York: E.P. Dutton & Co., Inc., 1975.

Miller, Don. *"B" Movies: An Informal Survey of the American Low-Budget Film, 1933–1945.* New York: Curtis Books, 1973.

Ramsaye, Terry. *1945–46 International Motion Picture Almanac.* New York: Quigley Publishing Company, 1945.

Index

Note: *Only those PRC films discussed in the text are indexed below. An alphabetical listing of these films appears under* Producers Releasing Corporation — Works. *Other PRC films may be found in the alphabetical checklist, pp. 98–148. A* **boldface** *page number indicates a photograph on that page.*

151